Western Apache Language and Culture

Western Apache Language and Culture

ESSAYS IN LINGUISTIC ANTHROPOLOGY

Keith H. Basso

THE UNIVERSITY OF ARIZONA PRESS   TUCSON & LONDON

The University of Arizona Press

Copyright © 1990
The Arizona Board of Regents
All Rights Reserved

This book was set in 9¹/₂ on 12¹/₂ Linotron Trump Mediaeval.
⊗ This book is printed on acid-free, archival-quality paper.
Manufactured in the United States of America.

97   96   95   5   4   3

Library of Congress Cataloging-in-Publication Data

Basso, Keith H., 1940–
    Western Apache language and culture : essays in linguistic
anthropology / Keith H. Basso.
        p.   cm.
    Includes bibliographical references.
    ISBN 0-8165-1323-6 (alk. paper)
    1. Western Apache language.   2. Western Apache Indians.
I. Title.
PM2583.B38   1989
497'.2—dc20   89-20242
                                                    CIP

British Library Cataloguing in Publication data are available.
A catalogue record of this book is available from the British Library.

For my mother, Etolia S. Basso

Contents

Figures   ix

Introduction   xi

Western Apache Pronunciation Guide   xix

1 / The Western Apache Classificatory Verb   1
     System: A Semantic Analysis

2 / Semantic Aspects of Linguistic Acculturation   15

3 / A Western Apache Writing System: 25
     The Symbols of Silas John

4 / 'Wise Words' of the Western Apache: Metaphor   53
     and Semantic Theory

5 / 'To Give Up on Words': Silence in Western   80
     Apache Culture

6 / 'Stalking with Stories': Names, Places, and   99
     Moral Narratives among the Western Apache

7 / 'Speaking with Names': Language and   138
     Landscape among the Western Apache

     Notes to Chapters   175

     References Cited   183

     Index   191

Figures

1. The semantic domain of Western Apache classifi-   11
   catory verb stems.
2. Treelike structure of verb stem domain as re-   12
   vealed by ordered application of semantic dimensions and features.
3. Western Apache anatomical terms with extended   17
   meanings.
4. Taxonomic structure of anatomical set.   20
5. Taxonomic structure of extended set.   21
6. Text of 'prayer for life' in correct reading form,   32
   from left to right in descending order.
7. Three texts of 'prayer for life', arranged in vertical   33
   order for ease of comparison.
8. Three texts of 'prayer for sickness', arranged in   34
   vertical order for ease of comparison.
9. Noncompound and compound symbols.   36
10. Symbols grouped into classes A, B, and C.   37
11. Formulas for the formation of types of compound   38
    symbols.
12. Lexical hierarchy showing location of Western   63
    Apache categories 'carrion beetle' (*koyiłchoozhé*)
    and 'white man' (*ndaa*).
13. Major categories of Western Apache speech.   114
14. Major categories of Western Apache narrative.   115
15. Major categories of Western Apache narrative dis-   116
    tinguished by temporal locus of events and pri-
    mary purposes of narration.

16. *t'iis bitł'áh tú 'olį́į́'* ('water flows inward under-   156
    neath a cottonwood tree').
17. *tsé łigai dah sidil* ('white rocks live above in a   157
    compact cluster').
18. *tsé biká' tú yahilį́į́'* ('water flows down on top of a   158
    regular succession of flat rocks').

Introduction

*The worlds men build are as varied as the tools with which
they build them, and since their primary tools are the
languages they speak, their worlds must be varied indeed.*

THEODORE RILKE

What can the study of spoken languages reveal about the shapes
and contours of other cultural worlds? And what can thus be
learned about improving the craft of ethnographic description?
In one form or another, these two questions have been part of
anthropology for the better part of a century. Yet despite their
venerable status, and notwithstanding exemplary efforts to address them in systematic terms, they continue to exert a compelling fascination. They are intricate questions, as complex
and multisided as the phenomena they embrace, and respond-
ing to them with sweeping abstractions has seldom proved successful. For by common consent the life of any language resides
in the welter of its myriad particulars—in the delicate symme-
tries of its grammatical structures and the subtle nuances of
even the most ordinary forms of speech—and so it is through
the investigation of small details, a slow and exacting business
at best, that solid advances most often get made. Regrettably
perhaps but necessarily nonetheless, linguistic anthropologists
are obliged to work in fairly constant miniature, and the larger
truths they manage to uncover, like certain costly gifts, tend to
come wrapped in modest-looking packages.

The essays contained in this volume are certainly modest
enough, and such truths as they present (or merely try to suggest, or only succeed at hinting at) are of complementary scope.
Written at irregular intervals during the past twenty-five years,
all the essays are trained on the language and culture of a single
American Indian tribe, the Western Apache of Arizona, but
their very different topics—a set of classificatory verbs, an un-

usual system of writing, the role of silence in verbal communication, and others—provide for considerable diversity.[1] As might be expected, this diversity is accompanied at points by shifts in theoretical orientation and interpretive approach—here the formalist framework of structural semantics and ethnographic lexicography, here the widened stance of interactional sociolinguistics, here again the self-reflexive attitude of recent work in symbolic analysis—the mixed result of a restless curiosity and the inexorable fact that the nature of one's subject matter makes certain approaches more suitable and effective than others. An eclectic volume, then, a series of anthropological feints and jabs (alas, there are no knock-out punches) which come at their targets from several distinct directions. And so, too, an "experimental" volume, at least in the sense of pursuing these directions into uncharted cultural territory, applying them there to bodies of rich empirical materials, and then attempting to clarify (more often by concrete example than extended logical argument) their value and utility for the discipline as a whole.

Although my work among the Western Apache has moved unpredictably from one arresting subject to the next, it has been steadily informed by a set of guiding assumptions which should here be made explicit. As I conceive of it, linguistic anthropology is a way of doing ethnography that seeks to interpret social and cultural systems through the manifold lenses afforded by language and speech. It proceeds on the premise that ethnographic fieldwork is centered on discerning the meanings of local symbolic forms, that language is everywhere a symbolic form without parallel or peer, and that the activity of speaking—of enacting and implementing language—is surely among the most meaning-filled of all. On such a view, language emerges as a powerful vehicle of thought and a crucial instrument for accomplishing social interaction, as an indispensable means of knowing the world and for performing deeds within it. Accordingly, the study of language structure (of grammatical forms, relations, and categories) joins with the study of language use (of situated communicative intentions and the multiple functions served by particular modes of speaking) in a manner that privileges neither, enlarges the scope of each, and throws sharp and vivid light on the sociocultural contexts of which both are products and expressions. Language and speech, distinguishable in theory but in life quite inseparable, two convergent streets that merge into one broad thoroughfare for engaging and exploring different versions of the world.

The world that I have explored most extensively is inhabited by Western Apache men and women who make their homes in Cibecue, a remote community located in a shallow mountain valley near the center of the Fort Apache Indian Reservation in east-central Arizona.[2] The fifteen hundred residents of Cibecue speak a dialect of Western Apache that is spoken nowhere else, and for this and other reasons they consider themselves distinct from people who live elsewhere on the Fort Apache reservation. They also set themselves apart on linguistic and cultural grounds from Apaches living on the San Carlos Apache Indian Reservation, the Tonto Apache Indian Reservation, and those who reside in smaller settlements near Camp Verde, Cottonwood, and Clarkdale. Despite these differences, I have no reason to believe that the factual matters taken up in these pages are either restricted to the Cibecue community or atypical of the Western Apache in general; indeed, I have been assured by a number of Apache consultants that they are not.

When I first went to Cibecue in 1959 (the population then stood at less than 825), Western Apache was the preferred language of everyone in the community except for a small knot of non-Indian traders, missionaries, and government employees. Today, thirty years later, the situation remains basically the same, although increasing numbers of younger Apaches (some of whom are fully and imaginatively bilingual) see fit on occasion to embellish their speech with English words and phrases. As one moves about the village, however, it is the native language one hears—in homes, in the trading post, at rodeos and religious events, even at the recently opened "commercial center" where revenues from the sale of television sets and video cassette recorders now rival those from soda pop, potatoes, and one-pound cans of coffee. Only in the local school (where English is the primary language of instruction) and the medical clinic (where its arcane use by Anglo physicians regularly baffles one and all) does the absence of spoken Apache create a strange and disquieting vacuum. Should that vacuum ever become permanent, the people of Cibecue will have lost one of their most cherished and beautiful possessions, and they will never be the same again. Mrs. Annie Peaches, my first Apache teacher and a woman of formidable intelligence, made this point in the strongest possible terms. "If we lose our language, we will lose our breath. Then we will die and blow away like leaves."

A member of the great Athabascan language family, Western Apache boasts a grammar of astonishing complexity, and nowhere is this more clearly apparent as in the area of verb morphology. A lexical unit of variable length, the Western Apache verb is composed of several morphological particles that combine to modify a verb stem, the latter acting as a sort of semantic anchor that fuses and unifies the construction as a whole. Chapter 1 offers a semantic analysis of a set of Apache "classificatory" verb stems, so called because they encode information about observable properties of the object or objects whose movement the verb describes. In various combinations, these attributes—length of object, rigidity, portability, etc.—define a bounded system of abstract conceptual categories which Apache speakers must learn if they are to use the stems correctly. Concomitantly, speakers are constrained to attend to particular attributes of objects as "significant" while ignoring others (such as color) as "insignificant," a revealing example of how grammatical structures may work to channel perception along highly specific lines.

Lexical structures may of course do likewise. By way of illustration, chapter 2 presents a discussion of the semantic domain delineated by Western Apache terms for the human body. The categories labeled by these terms are ordered by a series of increasingly restricted "part of" relationships (e.g., 'body' → 'arm' → 'hand'), a principle that organizes the whole domain into a multilevel hierarchy. When Apache people became familiar with automobiles in the 1930s, selected anatomical terms were extended to describe them, and this same form of hierarchical organization was transferred intact to the new domain of motorized vehicles. It remains intact today, a striking reminder that changes in the meanings of individual words may be accompanied by lasting continuities in their deeper structural relationships.

Scholars have classified writing systems in a variety of ways, but the script invented in 1904 by Silas John Edwards, a Western Apache religious leader, fits none of the standard typologies. Chapter 3, which seeks to make explicit the knowledge required to become literate in this script, begins by investigating Apache linguistic categories for distinguishing among different kinds of functionally significant graphs. Only when these distinctions are understood can one describe the rules that govern the combination of graphs into allowable sequences, and only then can one appreciate just what it is that makes the script unique. Used by Mr. Edwards and his followers to record a body of ceremonial prayers, the writing system embodies a precise mnemonic which specifies the performance of appropriate forms of nonverbal action as well as appropriate forms of ritual speech.

Everyday talk in Western Apache communities abounds with intricate tropes, yet even those that appear relatively uncomplicated—"Girls are butterflies," for example, or "Widows are ravens"—present large interpretive problems for the cultural outsider. Chapter 4 identifies some of these problems, examines them in relation to metaphorical expressions of the sort given above, and goes on to sketch the outlines of a general theory of figurative speech. It is suggested that such a theory should account for the manifest ability of language users to construct sense and significance from semantically ill-formed utterances (which metaphors commonly are), and that the crux of this ability consists in formulating novel concepts which facilitate the discovery of apt and useful truths in ostensibly false assertions.

While choosing not to speak is universally recognized as an effective communicative device, the interactional purposes to which silence is put may vary markedly from culture to culture. Although most Western Apaches take keen delight in the

pleasures of conversation, situations regularly arise when they
refrain from speech completely—a decision, they assert, that is
largely motivated by considerations of politeness and respect.
Chapter 5 describes these situations, mounts a search for
their common social denominators, and concludes that silence
among Apaches stems from perceptions of uncertainty and ambiguity in the organization of role relationships in face-to-face
encounters.

Much has been written about American Indian conceptions
of the natural environment and the great importance native
peoples attach to the lands on which they live. The Western
Apache are no exception in this regard, and chapters 6 and 7,
which examine the use of local placenames in two styles of contemporary discourse, attempt to indicate some of the reasons
why. Rejecting the view that Apache placenames function exclusively as vehicles of reference, chapter 6 discusses their role
in framing historical narratives which recount events of abiding
moral significance for members of the modern community.
Chapter 7 pursues this theme by considering a more specialized
kind of talk, normally reserved for consoling persons beset by
fear and anxiety, in which placenames are employed as substi-
tutes for narratives to evoke healing aspects of Apache ancestral wisdom. In both instances, placenames are interpreted as
highly charged cultural symbols that work to establish binding
ties between Apache people and specific features of their geographical landscape, a constantly resonating landscape whose
manifold meanings give shape and substance to the present by
infusing it with timeless verities rooted in the past.

And there, somewhat breathlessly, you have it—a variegated
lot of writings but not, I think, a dull one. This is because Western Apache people are hardly ever dull and neither are their
lives. Sharing in those lives for the past three decades has pro-
foundly affected my own, and I cannot find the words (in English or Apache) to properly express my gratitude to the persons
who have helped me with my work. Neither do I know how to
thank those whose abundant sensitivity and sheer good will—
bestowed during times of happiness as well as heavy sadness—
have become for me a permanent source of quiet inspiration.

The following people have given gifts far beyond repaying: Annie Peaches, Calvert and Darlene Tessay, Dick Cooley, Don Cooley, Karen Tessay, Norma Jean Tessay, Teddy Peaches, Nashley Tessay, Sr., Morley Cromwell, Ernest Murphy, Charles Henry, Helena Henry, Robert and Lola Machuse, Nick Thompson, Nelson Lupe, Ronnie Lupe, Leon Beatty, Nora Gregg, Roy and Nannie Quay, Alvin Quay, Ervin Quay, Imogene Quay, Emily Quay, Dudley Patterson, Emerson Patterson, Frances and Sarah DeHose, Delmar Boni, Vincent Randall, Ned and Delphine Anderson, Philip Cassadore, Marlowe Cassadore, and Silas John Edwards.

Gifts have come from members of the scholarly community as well—from teachers Clyde Kluckhohn and Evon Z. Vogt (who encouraged my interests in linguistics and anthropology), Charles Frake and Roy D'Andrade (who broadened and cultivated them in graduate school), and from Dell Hymes, Clifford Geertz, and Erving Goffman (who later on provided a veritable stream of fresh ideas with which to pursue them further). I have also been richly instructed by the exemplary work and cordial critical comments of Harry Hoijer, Floyd Lounsbury, Morris Opler, Mary Haas, Sir Edmund Leach, Harry Basehart, Victor Turner, Ward Goodenough, David Schneider, Harold Conklin, Alton Becker, Raymond Thompson, John Gumperz, Scott Momaday, Brent Berlin, William Geohegan, Karen Blu, Joel Sherzer, Richard Bauman, Regna Darnell, Larry Evers, Michael Silverstein, Steven Feld, William Hanks, Alfonso Ortiz, Ray McDermott, Bill Douglas, William Longacre, Scott Rushforth, Philip Greenfeld, and Michael Graves. It is a singular pleasure to thank them all.

And then there is Vine Deloria, Jr. Purveyor of biting wit and gentle sagacity alike, his deeply moral voice has done more than any other to create the ethical and political climate in which students of American Indian cultures today must ply their trade. Though no great fan of anthropologists, he has contributed a great deal to the education of this one—not only where Native Americans are concerned, but also, and with equal gusto, on matters pertaining to loyal dogs, marginal poker hands, advancing age, self-absorbed intellectuals, weak defensive secondaries, and the complex metaphysics of old songs by Gene Autry. I salute him and thank him for his friendship.

The essays assembled here grew out of fieldwork funded by the National Science Foundation, the National Institutes of Mental Health, the American Philosophical Society, the Wenner-Gren Foundation for Anthropological Research, Inc., the Center for the Study of Man (Smithsonian Institution), the University of Arizona Research Foundation, the Doris Duke American Indian Oral History Project, and the J. T. Vance Foundation (Tucson, Arizona). Needless to say, I am grateful to these organizations for their support. I should also like to acknowledge the American Anthropological Association, the American Association for the Advancement of Science, the *Journal of Anthropological Research*, and the University of New Mexico Press, all of whom gave permission to reprint one or more of the essays in modified form. In preparing a final "electronic manuscript" of the anthology for the University of Arizona Press, June-el Piper proceeded with such expert efficiency as to make a difficult job look almost easy.

My wife, Gayle Potter-Basso, whose own ethnographic work with Western Apache people has made her my most informed and trenchant critic, knows better than anyone who made possible the completion of this book. My mother, Etolia S. Basso, to whom the book is dedicated, knows what has gone into it. These two ladies, along with Margie and certain other independent spirits who flourish on the Halter Cross Ranch, make everything lively and worthwhile.

KEITH H. BASSO

Western Apache
Pronunciation Guide

The Western Apache language contains four vowels:

a—as in "father"

e—as in "red"

i—as in "police"

o—as in "go" (varying toward *u* as in "to")

All of the four vowels may be pronounced short or long, depending on duration of sound. Vowel length is indicated typographically with double vowels (e.g., *aa*).

Each of the vowels may be nasalized. This is indicated by a subscript hook placed under the vowel (e.g., *ą* and *ąą*). In pronouncing a nasalized vowel, air passes through the nasal passage so as to give the vowel a soft, slightly ringing sound.

The four Western Apache vowels may also be pronounced with high or low tone. High tone is indicated by an accent mark over the vowel (e.g., *á*), showing that the vowel is pronounced with a rising pitch. In certain instances, the consonant *ń* is also spoken with high tone.

Western Apache contains approximately thirty-one consonants and consonant clusters. Fifteen of these are pronounced approximately as in English: *b, d, ch, h, j, k, l, m, n, s, sh, t, w, y, z.*

Another consonant in Western Apache is the *glottal stop.* Indicated by an apostrophe ('), the glottal stop may occur before and after all four vowels and after certain consonants and consonant clusters. Produced by closure of the glottis so as to momentarily halt air passing through the mouth, the glottal stop resembles the interruption of breath one hears between the two "ohs" in the English expression "oh-oh." The glottalized consonants and consonant clusters in Western Apache are *k'*, *t'*, *ch'*, *tł'*, *and ts'*.

Other consonants and consonant clusters include:

dl—as in the final syllable of "paddling"

dz—as in the final sound of "adds"

g—as in "get" (never as in "gentle")

gh—similar to *g* but pronounced farther back in the mouth, this consonant often sounds like a gutteral *w*

hw—as in "what"

kw—as in "quick"

ł—This consonant, sometimes called the "silent *l*," has no counterpart in English. The mouth is shaped for *l* but the vocal cords are not used. The sound is made by expelling air from both sides of the tongue.

tł—as in "Tlingit"

ts—as in the final sound of "pots"

zh—as in "azure"

Western Apache Language and Culture

1 / The Western Apache Classificatory Verb System: A Semantic Analysis

All Athabascan languages for which reliable data are available have been found to contain classificatory verb stems. As Harry Hoijer (1945) and other investigators have pointed out, these sets of morphemes do not distinguish among categories of events (as do many Athabascan verbs) but among categories of objects instead. For example, in Western Apache the stems -*tįįh* and -*áh* are found in expressions such as *nát'oh shantįįh* and *nát'oh shan'áh*, both of which may be loosely interpreted as "Hand me the tobacco." The difference in meaning between the verbs in these expressions is signaled by their respective stems: *shantįįh* specifies that a single elongated object is to be handled, while *shan'áh* specifies that the object is squarish and compact. The two verb stems thus identify different referents of the noun *nát'oh* ('tobacco'), indicating in this manner that the first expression is properly interpreted as "Hand me the cigarette" (or perhaps a cigar), the second as "Hand me the pack of cigarettes" (or perhaps a pouch of chewing tobacco).[1]

As this example shows, selections among alternate Western Apache verb stems are governed not by grammatical rules but by extralinguistic considerations, that is, by physical properties of the object or objects to which a speaker refers. In this regard, the use of verb stems is analogous to that of many Apache nouns: the speaker takes note of an object, determines on the basis of certain properties that it belongs to a particular category, and labels it accordingly with the appropriate linguistic form. In so doing, and typically quite unconsciously, he or she classifies a portion of the environment along culturally determined lines.

Mary Haas (1967) has observed that the study of classificatory verb stems may be of considerable value in disclosing the form and structure of "covert cultural taxonomies," which she defines as taxonomies whose constituent categories are labeled by linguistic units operating at "sub-lexemic" levels. She also notes, however, that studies based on large samples of category instances are generally lacking, and that important questions concerning the definition of individual categories need to be addressed. The Western Apache classificatory verb system, which is here described for the first time, provides a felicitous opportunity to deal with these issues and see where they may lead.

Defining Verb Stem Categories

How are the categories distinguished by classificatory verb stems to be discovered and defined? A common procedure has been to choose some set of objects as typical of a particular category, construct a characterization of their salient properties, and offer this characterization as a definition of the category as a whole. This procedure, which may be called *definition by typification,* has been employed to define the object categories of Navajo as well as those of a number of other Athabascan languages (Davidson et al. 1963). Thus, one Navajo category is defined as "a fabriclike object" (e.g., a blanket, an article of clothing, or a piece of paper), another as "a bulky object" (e.g., a heavy box, crate, or bundle), and so on. Although definitions of this sort are helpful in conveying an intuitive sense of what sorts of objects can be included in a verb stem category, they fail to make explicit the necessary and sufficient conditions for category membership. This is not a trivial shortcoming. On the contrary, I found in my research that the diversity of objects included in certain Western Apache categories made it impossible to define them with simple characterizations such as "bulky" and "fabriclike." Such characterizations were either too general or not general enough; they were vague, ambiguous, and in some cases seriously misleading.

In an effort to overcome these difficulties, I turned to the method of componential analysis.[2] The basic objective of a componential analysis is to provide each member of a set of linguistically coded categories with a unique *definition by signification*. Such definitions are typically expressed as a list or bundle of semantic features that specify the criteria according to which items are included in (and excluded from) the categories in question. Ideally at least, such definitions are also unitary or "conjunctive" in that they present a single set of criteria for category membership and do not propose alternatives. The steps required to arrive at definitions by signification (also called componential definitions) may be briefly summarized as follows. First, a record is made of items that native speakers claim a linguistic form may denote; these items comprise that form's *denotata*. The next step is to adduce the form's *significata*, the features of meaning which together serve to distinguish it from every other form. This is accomplished by a combination of two operations: (1) inspecting the form's denotata for shared attributes, and (2) contrasting these attributes with those adduced from inspection of the denotata of all other forms.

The data for this study were provided by three Apache consultants, all of them male and over sixty years of age, who live in the community of Cibecue. Each consultant was presented with a set of eliciting frames containing verbs that require the use of a classificatory verb stem. The frames also contained a position or slot in which consultants were required to substitute a noun that labeled a category of objects. (To give an example, in the frame *X shan-Y* ['Hand me X'], *X* represents the noun slot and *Y* the slot for a verb stem.) My consultants repeated these frames many times, on each occasion supplying a different noun and, when it was called for, a different classificatory stem. In this way I was able to record extensive sets of Apache nouns whose referents, by virtue of having occurred with a specific stem, could be treated as that stem's denotata.

Native interpretations concerning verb stem category criteria were secured in the following manner. When a sufficient number of denotata had been obtained for a particular verb stem, I asked my Apache consultants to comment on whether these objects were similar or different. Similarity was emphasized in case after case and was readily explained with such statements as "Those (things) are all long" and "Those (things) don't bend." A second and more interesting task, which stressed intercategory differences rather than intracategory similarities, required consultants to compare the denotata of two or more verb stems and to specify the grounds on which they were dissimilar. This procedure, which yielded such assertions as "Those (things) are long and those aren't" and "Those (things) bend but those don't," was particularly helpful when native ideas concerning category criteria differed from my own.

As I hope to illustrate below, the method of componential analysis proved an effective aid in defining Western Apache classificatory verb stem categories. I was able to assign conjunctive definitions to all but one of these categories, the exception being a category that Apaches themselves recognize as containing a disjunction and acknowledge to be atypical in this respect. Although I would not claim that the interpretation presented here is entirely free of ambiguity, it does show that definitions by typification can obscure important aspects of classificatory verb stem systems, and that the method of componential analysis is potentially applicable to such systems wherever they are found.

Verb Stem Denotata

I present here the thirteen classificatory verb stems of Western Apache, together with partial inventories of their respective denotata.

CATEGORY I (*-tįįh*): Pencil, pen, hunting knife, folding (or pocket) knife, crowbar, wood rasp, metal file, one-handled wood saw, two-handled wood saw, length of iron pipe, cigarette, cigar, match, fork, spoon, rake, shovel, hoe, pickaxe, axe, hatchet, car key, rifle, shotgun, metal or wooden ruler, carpenter's T-square, carpenter's level, metal bolt, nail, screw, wire brad, baseball bat, flashlight, hammer, wrench, piece of firewood, cradleboard, clothespin, arrow shaft, bow, fence post, blade of grass, log.

CATEGORY II (*-'áh*): Pail, washbasin, drinking glass, coffee cup, frying pan, kerosene can, tin can (all sizes), shoe, boot, spool of thread, spool of wire, cake of soap, loaf of bread, box of detergent soap, box of matches, package of cigarettes, package of cigars, package of chewing tobacco, automobile tire, truck tire, chair, table, light bulb, kerosene lantern, brick, book, egg, slab of bacon (unsliced), apple, peach, pear, potato, acorn, piñon nut, walnut, peanut, all nonpaper money (i.e., coins), cigarette lighter, beer bottle, wine bottle, milk container, burden basket, flat basket, flashlight battery, wallet, Dutch oven, coffee pot, revolver, pocket watch, shoebox, saddle, cooking tin, kernel of corn, grain of salt, oil or gasoline drum, bale of hay, pebble.

CATEGORY III (*-tsoos*): Piece of paper, blanket, horse blanket, saddle pad, pillow case, sleeping bag, buckskin, trousers, T-shirt, shirt, all paper money (i.e., bills), tortilla, paper sack, burlap sack (feed sack), sock, towel, piece of canvas, piece of roofing paper, brassiere, woman's slip, woman's dress, diaper, sweater, pillow.

CATEGORY IV (*-léh*): Piece of rope, lasso, piece of string, piece of thread, shoestring, piece of fishline, piece of rawhide, strip of buckskin, saddle cinch, saddle girth, belt (leather, rope, or twine), horse collar, bridle rein, electrical extension cord, automobile fan belt, wire cable, rubber band, strip of tape, strand of hair, rubber hose, metal chain.

Plus *two* of any item listed above, or *two* of any item in categories I, II, and III. From a total of 126 denotata recorded for the dual component of this category, I present here a representative sample of twenty-five.

Two pieces of rope, two pieces of string, two saddle cinches, two bridle reins, two lengths of rubber hose, two metal chains.

Two pencils, two pens, two metal files, two cigarettes, two matches, two rifles, two arrow shafts.

Two pails, two drinking glasses, two boots, two walnuts, two flashlight batteries, two pocket watches, two packages of cigarettes.

Two pieces of paper, two blankets, two buckskins, two T-shirts, two tortillas, a pair of socks.

CATEGORY V (*-diił*): *More than two* of any item in category I. For example (from a recorded total of 49 denotata), 3 pencils, 4 pens, 4 hunting knives, 5 rifles, 8 matches, 12 cigarettes, 37 nails, 45 metal bolts, a handful of screws, a pile of hay, a stack of fence posts, 17 arrow shafts, 6 shovels, 4 axes.

CATEGORY VI (*-jáh*): *More than two* of any item in category II. For example (from a recorded total of 98 denotata), 3 pails, 4 kerosene lanterns, 5 loaves of bread, 10 packages of cigarettes, 24 boxes of matches, a handful of coins, 24 flashlight batteries, 12 burden baskets, 8 eggs, 11 apples, 5 cigarette lighters.

CATEGORY VII (*-né'*): *More than two* of any item in category III, and *more than two* of any item which, when spoken of in the singular, belongs to category IV. For example (from a recorded total of 61 denotata), 3 pieces of paper, a stack of 6 tortillas, 8 T-shirts, a pile of blankets, 14 burlap sacks (feed sacks), a pile of diapers, 7 towels, 3 dresses.

Three pieces of rope, 6 shoestrings, 8 bridle reins, a pile of metal chains, a handful of threads.

CATEGORY VIII (*-tɫeeh*): Mud, wet clay, oatmeal (in its prepared form), baking dough, ice cream, wet adobe.

CATEGORY IX (*-ziig*): Water, coffee (in its fluid form), soda pop, beer, wine, whiskey, gasoline, kerosene, motor oil, milk, chocolate milk, tea (in fluid form), soup, broth, stew, tulipai (a mild native liquor).

CATEGORY X (*-kaah*): Any item (or items) in categories I, II, III, IV (singular component), VIII, and IX when these are contained in any of the following: a cup, a washbasin, a drinking glass, a cooking pot, a coffee pot, a bowl, a washtub, a basket, a gasoline can, a milk carton, a milk can, a bottle, a canteen, a cardboard box, a suitcase. For example (from a recorded total of 67 denotata): a cup of nails, a cup of corn kernels, a cup of sugar, a glass containing coins, a glass containing cigarettes, a basket containing clothes, a basket containing papers, a suitcase full of string, a milk carton containing mud, a pot containing coffee, a bowl containing stew.

CATEGORY XI (*-dęh*): Any item (or items) in categories I, II, III, IV (singular component), VIII, and IX when these are contained in any of the following: a paper bag, a burlap sack (feed sack), a plasticene bag, a blanket (folded over and around its contents so as to make a "bundle"), a buckskin (folded in the manner of a blanket), a shirt or dress (folded in the manner of a blanket), a newspaper. For example (from a recorded total of 75 denotata): a paper bag containing pencils, a paper bag containing nails, a paper bag containing cigarettes, a paper bag containing acorns, a paper bag containing coins, a paper bag containing T-shirts, a paper bag containing rawhide thongs, a plasticene bag containing water, a blanket "bundle" containing groceries, a plasticene bag containing mud, a buckskin "bundle" containing feathers.

CATEGORY XII (-*teeh*): Puppy, mature dog, kitten, mature cat, chicken, turkey, calf, colt, fawn (deer), trout, water snake, earthworm, moth, caterpillar, butterfly, bobcat, javelina (peccary), goat, human infant.

CATEGORY XIII (-*lǫǫs*): Heifer, steer, cow, bull, horse, pig (adult), deer (adult), elk, bear, mule, burro, mountain lion, adult human.

Semantic Dimensions and Category Definitions

Seven semantic dimensions, marked by sixteen associated features, are required to define in necessary and sufficient terms the categories labeled by Western Apache classificatory verb stems.[3]

A. ANIMAL/NONANIMAL. There are two features on this dimension: "animal" and "nonanimal." The former, designated by the symbol (a_1), includes all vertebrates and insects. The latter, designated (a_2), includes flora, liquids, minerals, and practically all items of material culture.

B. ENCLOSURE. There are two features on this dimension. The first (b_1) refers to the condition whereby an item or object is enclosed in a container. The second (b_2) refers to the condition whereby it is not enclosed.

C. STATE. There are three features on this dimension: "solid" (c_1), "plastic" (c_2), and "liquid" (c_3). The second feature refers to malleable substances, such as mud, wet clay, etc., and might also have been defined as "neither solid nor liquid."

D. NUMBER. There are three features on this dimension: "one" (d_1), "two" (d_2), and "more than two" (d_3).

E. RIGIDITY. There are two features on this dimension: "rigid" (e_1) and "nonrigid" (e_2). The Apache consider an object to be rigid (*ntłiz*) if, when held at its edge or end, it does not bend.

F. LENGTH. There are two features on this dimension. The first (f_1) refers to the condition whereby the horizontal length of an object is at least *three times greater* than either its width or its height. The second feature (f_2) refers to the condition whereby the length of an object is *less* than three times its width or height.

G. PORTABILITY. There are two features on this dimension: "portable" (g_1) and "nonportable" (g_2). The former refers to items that are light enough to be easily carried by one person. The latter refers to items sufficiently heavy to require at least two persons to carry them.

Having postulated this set of semantic dimensions and features, the thirteen Western Apache verb stem categories may now be separately defined. As noted above, this is accomplished by assigning to each of the categories a list of features that specifies its membership criteria.

CATEGORY I (*-tįįh*): a_2 b_2 c_1 d_1 e_1 f_1. This expression is to be read as follows. Category I includes single, solid, nonanimal objects, unenclosed in a container, that are rigid and whose length is at least three times greater than their width or height. As can be seen, most of the objects in this category are tools and with only a few exceptions (e.g., cigarettes and cigars) are made of metal or wood.

CATEGORY II (*-'áh*): a_2 b_2 c_1 d_1 e_1 f_2. Category II includes single, solid, nonanimal objects, unenclosed in a container, that are rigid and whose length is *less* than three times as great as their width or height. It is this last feature—relative length—that distinguishes category II from category I. Of all the categories that refer to single objects, category II is the most inclusive; it encompasses the vast majority of items of material culture.

CATEGORY III (*-tsoos*): a_2 b_2 c_1 d_1 e_2 f_2. Category III includes single, solid, nonanimal objects, unenclosed in a container, that are *not rigid* and whose length is less than three times as great as their width or height. Category III contrasts with category II solely on the dimension of rigidity; otherwise the two are identical. With two or three exceptions (e.g., tortilla, buckskin), all the objects in category III are manufactured from paper or cloth. CATEGORY IV (*-léh*): IVa—a_2 b_2 c_1 d_1 e_2 f_1; IVb—a_2 b_2 c_1 d_2. This is the only stem for which I was unable to formulate a conjunctive definition. In the sense specified by definition IVa it refers to single, solid, nonanimal objects, unenclosed in a container, that are not rigid and whose length is at least three times greater than their width or height; in this sense it contrasts minimally—on the dimension of rigidity—with category I. According to definition IVb, *-léh* may also refer to *two* solid, nonanimal objects (regardless of length or rigidity), unenclosed in a container, including those specified by definition IVa and also those in categories I, II, and III.

The disjunction in category IV is not indicative of a failure of method; rather, it is a natural property of the stem in question. This conclusion is strengthened by two sets of evidence. First, all my Apache consultants were quick to point out that, unlike other stems, *-léh* had both a singular and a dual component. A typical comment was that it could refer either to "one thing, like a rope or string" (see definition IVa) or to "two things, many kinds" (see definition IVb). Second, and perhaps more telling, is the fact that precisely the same disjunction is contained in classificatory verb stems of other Apachean languages. For example, in Navajo, just as in Western Apache, "sets of two" and "ropelike objects" are consistently grouped together (Davidson et al. 1963:32).

It is interesting to note that because of its disjunctive character category IV is slightly ambiguous; it is impossible to tell from the stem alone whether a speaker is referring to a single object of the type specified in definition IVa or to two of them (IVb).

CATEGORY V (*-diił*): a_2 b_2 c_1 d_3 e_1 f_1. Category V includes *more than two* solid, nonanimal objects, unenclosed in a container, that are rigid and whose length is at least three times greater than their width or height. This category contrasts with category I only on the basis of number.

CATEGORY VI (*-jáh*): a_2 b_2 c_1 d_3 e_1 f_2. Category VI includes *more than two* solid, nonanimal objects, unenclosed in a container, that are rigid and whose length is *less* than three times as great as their width or height. Note that with respect to categories V and VI the dimension of rigidity is noncriterial. These categories contrast only on the dimension of length.

CATEGORY VII (*-né'*): a_2 b_2 c_1 d_3 e_2. Category VII includes *more than two* solid, nonanimal objects, unenclosed in a container, that are *not* rigid.

CATEGORY VIII (*-tɬeeh*): a_2 b_2 c_2. Category VIII includes objects best described as masses or conglomerates of nonanimal plastic material, unenclosed in a container. The number of items in this category is quite limited. It is used most frequently to refer to lumps of mud, clay, and baking dough.

CATEGORY IX (*-ziig*): a_2 b_2 c_3. Category IX includes liquid substances but *not* their containers. My consultants stated explicitly that to comprehend this category it was helpful to "think like there's nothing around it (the liquid)" or, alternatively, to "forget it's in something." It is in this sense, then, of liquids conceptualized as *independent* of their retaining vessels, that the feature "uncontained" is used to define category IX. The significance of this distinction, perhaps somewhat ambiguous with respect to liquids, will become apparent in the discussion of categories X and XI.

CATEGORY X (*-kaah*): a_2 b_1 e_1. Category X includes nonanimal objects—regardless of state, length, rigidity, or number—that are enclosed in *rigid containers*. Here it is critical to understand that reference is made to both a container *and* its contents and not, as in category IX, to contents alone. Notice, too, that in the definition given above "rigidity" describes an attribute of containers and not (necessarily) their contents.

CATEGORY XI (*-dęh*): a_2 b_1 e_2. Category XI includes nonanimal objects—regardless of state, length, rigidity, or number—that are enclosed in *nonrigid* containers. Just as in category X, container and contents are here conceptualized as an undifferentiated unit, unlike category IX where they are regarded as separate and independent. Categories X and XI are identical except

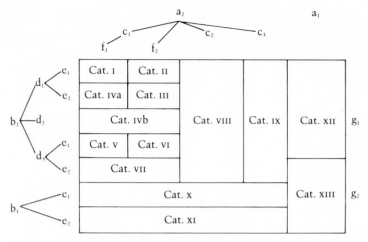

FIGURE I. The semantic domain of Western Apache classificatory verb stems.

for a minimal contrast on the dimension of container rigidity.

CATEGORY XII (*-teeh*): a_1 g_1. Category XII includes animals that are light enough to be easily lifted and transported by one person.

CATEGORY XIII (*-lǫǫs*): a_2 g_2. Category XIII includes animals that are too heavy to be easily lifted and carried by a single person.[4]

The Structure of the Verb Stem Domain

In considering each of the Western Apache verb stem categories separately, it is easy to lose sight of their structural relationships vis-à-vis one another. These relationships are illustrated in figure I, which represents the conceptual domain delineated by the entire set of verb stems. What is not shown in figure I is that the semantic dimensions and features that structure the domain have a probable ordering, thus making their application obligatory in the treelike sequence depicted in figure 2.[5] Thus, when selecting a verb stem, an Apache speaker must first determine whether an object is an animal; if it is not an animal, is the object enclosed or not; if it is not enclosed, is the object

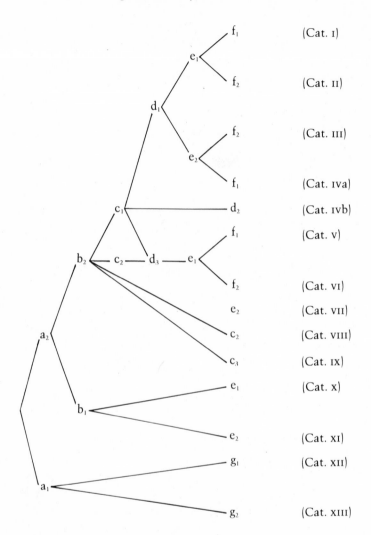

FIGURE 2. Treelike structure of verb stem domain as revealed by
ordered application of semantic dimensions and features.

solid, plastic, or liquid; if it is solid then is it singular, dual, or plural; if singular, is it rigid or flexible; and finally, if rigid, is its length three times greater than its width. If it is, the verb stem to use is *-tįįh*; if not, the appropriate stem is *-áh*.

Object Universals?

This study demonstrates that the procedures of componential analysis may be fruitfully applied to the description and interpretation of classificatory verb systems. Whether all classificatory verb systems will submit to these procedures remains to be seen, but it seems unlikely that the Western Apache case is unique. Besides being more explicit than definitions based on category typifications, componential definitions are more susceptible to productive generalization. That is, if accurately formulated, componential definitions enable us to assign previously unencountered objects to their appropriate categories, presumably on the basis of information similar to that processed by native speakers. Finally, since a complete set of componential definitions attempts to specify *all* the dimensions of contrast within a semantic domain (something definitions by typification are not apt to do), the internal structure of that domain can be portrayed with greater clarity.

As Charles Frake (1962) and Eugene Hammel (1964) have pointed out, an essential requirement for any kind of componential analysis is the availability of an adequate "metalanguage" with which analogous categories from different languages can be defined and compared. Such a metalanguage has been devised for the study of kinship terminologies, and one of the things it indicates is that the number of semantic dimensions required to define kinship categories is probably quite small. This may be true of classificatory verb stem categories as well. It is possible, of course, that the relatively few dimensions thus far reported for Athabascan languages can be explained as a result of their close genetic relationship. However, studies of classificatory verb systems in non-Athabascan languages suggest that such systems may everywhere be structured by limited sets of similar semantic dimensions: animateness, state, number, length, rigidity, and the like. If this turns out to be the case, constructing an object category metalanguage that can be applied across unrelated languages should be feasible. It should also be extremely worthwhile, for it could lead eventually to the discovery and documentation of true "object universals." What is needed now is further research with an eye toward this objective.

2 / Semantic Aspects of Linguistic Acculturation

Language is a notoriously flexible instrument that registers changes in the content of cultural systems more sensitively and surely than any other. Such changes may affect phonetics, syntax, and vocabulary, but it is in the lexicon that they can be traced most readily, whether they are due to internal cultural developments or to the effects of intercultural contact. And yet in recent years the topic of vocabulary shifts has received little attention from anthropologists interested in processes of acculturation. For the most part, earlier studies of this phenomenon have focused upon the interrelationship of sociocultural and linguistic factors, with emphasis placed mainly on the former; and in those cases where linguistic factors have been stressed, phonetics and word morphology tend to receive much fuller treatment than semantics. In view of these circumstances, it seems both desirable and worthwhile to address the topic of lexical change anew.

The development of ethnographic lexicography has provided linguistic anthropologists with orderly procedures for describing taxonomic structures underlying native terminologies. Thus far, however, work in this area has dealt almost exclusively with synchronic aspects of terminological systems. In this chapter, I shall attempt to show that several concepts employed in lexicographical studies may be usefully brought to bear upon a type of semantic change that occurs as a result of intercultural contact. In so doing, I shall present and interpret a body of data collected among the Western Apache of Arizona.

First, however, it is necessary to consider a more traditional approach to the study of semantic change. In the past, shifts in the referential meaning of words have been described by (1) establishing the original meaning or primary sense of a given lexeme; (2) recording the changes that have altered this meaning; and (3) relating these changes to some set of linguistic, social, or historical factors that presumably precipitated them. In short, the basic procedure has been the documentation of a lexeme's history, conceived as a linear succession of units of meaning. This approach, which Stephen Ullman (1963) has aptly labeled "atomistic," rests on the assumption that while synchronic linguistics properly deals with systems, diachronic linguistics must concern itself with single elements. In the sphere of semantics, this assumption carries with it a strong implication that changes in the meaning of words typically occur independently of one another or, at best, are rarely systemically related. The atomistic approach thus raises a question of some importance: namely, is it possible to formulate descriptive generalizations about changes in referential meaning above the level of the isolated lexeme? I hope to show that such statements can be made and that they serve to clarify an intriguing form of linguistic acculturation that until recently has remained obscure.

There appear to be three major processes by which the vocabulary of a language adjusts to objects and ideas introduced as a consequence of intercultural contact. First, one or more lexemes—loanwords—may be borrowed from the language (or languages) associated with the alien culture. Second, new lexemes may be created from indigenous linguistic materials. Third, existing lexemes may be extended to label unfamiliar phenomena, thereby acquiring novel meanings that serve to enlarge their semantic range. The literature on loanwords is now quite voluminous (cf. Haugen 1956; Weinreich 1953), but processes of lexical innovation and extension have stimulated comparatively little research. It is the latter of these processes—lexical extension—that I wish to consider here.

Data from a modern Western Apache speech community in-

ANATOMICAL TERMS (re: humans)	EXTENDED MEANINGS (re: motorized vehicles)
biwos ('shoulder')	'front fender(s)'
bigan ('hand and arm')	'front wheel(s)', 'tires'
biyedaa' ('chin and jaw')	'front bumper'
bikee' ('foot', 'feet')	'rear wheels', 'tires'
bínii' ('face')	'area extending from top of windshield to front bumper'
bita' ('forehead')	'windshield'
bichįh ('nose')	'hood'
bigháń ('back')	'bed of truck'
bik'ai ('hip and buttock')	'rear fender(s)'
bizé' ('mouth')	'opening of pipe to gas tank'
bidáá ('eyes')	'headlights'
bits'ǫǫs ('veins')	'electrical wiring'
bibiiye' ('innards')	'all items under hood'
bizig ('liver')	'battery'
bibid ('stomach')	'gas tank'
bijíí ('heart')	'distributor'
bijíí'izólé ('lung')	'radiator'
bich'í' ('intestines')	'radiator hose(s)'
bi'ik'ah ('fat')	'grease'

FIGURE 3. Western Apache anatomical terms with extended meanings.

dicate that several decades ago a sizeable set of Apache lexemes was extended en masse to cover a conspicuous item of material culture introduced by Anglo-Americans. Specifically, a group of Apache anatomical terms was extended to label the different parts of automobiles and pickup trucks (see figure 3). As we shall see, the application of anatomical terms to motorized vehicles resulted in a kind of semantic change that is clearly apparent at the level of the terminological set but not at the level of its constituent lexemes. Consequently, a conventional atomistic interpretation—that is, an interpretation that examined the Apache terms in isolation and did not consider their relationships vis-à-vis one another—would fail to disclose that together with the individual lexemes a *system of classification* had also been extended. Following a closer look at the Apache data, I shall return to this point and discuss it in greater detail.

Anatomical Terms and Automobiles

Western Apache is one of seven languages that comprise the Southern Athabascan, or Apachean, substock of the Athabascan family. The other languages in this substock are Navajo, Chiricahua, Mescalero, Jicarilla, Lipan, and Kiowa-Apache. Western Apache includes five mutually intelligible dialects: San Carlos, Cibecue, White Mountain, and Northern and Southern Tonto (Goodwin 1942). Phonological differences between the San Carlos and White Mountain dialects have been described by Hill (1963). The material for this paper was provided by consultants living in the community at Cibecue, which is located just south of the Mogollon Rim near the center of the Fort Apache Indian Reservation.

My data come from five Apache men, sixty years or older, who speak but little English. All were present on the Fort Apache reservation between 1930 and 1935, when Apaches first began acquiring automobiles and pickup trucks. Unlike younger Apaches, some of whom are bilingual, my consultants were totally unfamiliar with English terms for the parts of motorized vehicles. This is not to suggest, however, that the use of extended anatomical terms is today restricted to members of the senior generation. On the contrary, the extended terminology is part of every Apache's basic vocabulary and is commonly resorted to in daily conversation. Long before an Apache child learns that a car has a battery, he or she knows it has a 'liver'.

Western Apache anatomical terms occur as responses to the query, *X bits'i la' hat'íí wolzee?* ('What are the parts of an *X*'s body called?'), where *X* is a lexeme labeling the class of objects whose anatomy is being investigated. Several hundred lexemes, including *naɬbiil* ('automobile', 'pickup truck'), can fill this position, and strictly speaking there are as many sets of anatomical terms as there are substitutable lexemes. The set that refers to 'humans' (*ndee*), for example, cannot be considered semantically isomorphic with the sets for 'horse' (*łįį*), 'bear' (*shash*), or 'automobile' (*nałbiil*), even though many of the same terms are present in all four. This becomes evident when we recognize that, depending on which set it is in, the same anatomical term may have distinctly different referents. Thus, applied to humans, the term *bikee'* denotes 'foot'; applied to horses, 'hoof'; to bears, 'paw'; and to automobiles, 'tires'.

In the presence of multiple anatomical sets, we can only speculate on which one, or ones, actually served as the model for labeling motorized vehicles. Several Apaches, citing functional similarities between cars and horses, suggested that the latter may have served in this capacity. Significantly, however, none of the anatomical terms extended to motorized vehicles is unique to the set for horses. In fact, the extended terms are found in a great many anatomical sets and so are extremely common. With this in mind, I shall concentrate on the set that is probably basic to all the others, that which is used in reference to men and women.

Listed in the left-hand column of figure 3 are nineteen anatomical terms supplied by my consultants in response to the query, *ndee bits'í la' hat'íí wolzee?* ('What are the parts of a person's body called?'). These lexemes, together with a large number of others that were not extended to automobiles, comprise what I shall call the *anatomical set*. The meanings of the extended terms, which are glossed in the right-hand column, were given in response to the query, *nałbííl bits'y 'a' hat'íí wolzee?* ('What are the parts of an automobile's body called?') and together make up the *extended set*. As shown in figure 4, the anatomical set takes the form of a three-level part-whole taxonomy, with *ndee bits'í* ('human's body') serving as the cover term. Eight of the set's eighteen remaining terms are subsumed under two superordinate lexemes, *binii'* ('face') and *bibiiye'* ('innards'), which operate at the second taxonomic level. It is important to note that the hierarchical structure of the anatomical set has been faithfully duplicated in the extended set. Indeed, as shown in figure 5 the two structures are identical.

bi'ik'ah ('fat')		*ndee bits'í* ('man's body')
biyedaa' ('chin and jaw')		*ndee bits'í* ('man's body')
biwos ('shoulder')		*ndee bits'í* ('man's body')
bigan ('hand and arm')		*ndee bits'í* ('man's body')
bik'ai ('hip and buttock')		*ndee bits'í* ('man's body')
bizé' ('mouth')		*ndee bits'í* ('man's body')
bikee' ('foot')		*ndee bits'í* ('man's body')
bighą́ń ('back')		*ndee bits'í* ('man's body')
bidą́ą́' ('eye')		*ndee bits'í* ('man's body')
bichį́h ('nose')	*binii'* ('face')	*ndee bits'í* ('man's body')
bita' ('forehead')	*binii'* ('face')	*ndee bits'í* ('man's body')
bits'ǫǫs ('vein')	*bibiiye'* ('innards')	*ndee bits'í* ('man's body')
bizig ('liver')	*bibiiye'* ('innards')	*ndee bits'í* ('man's body')
bibid ('stomach')	*bibiiye'* ('innards')	*ndee bits'í* ('man's body')
bich'í' ('intestine')	*bibiiye'* ('innards')	*ndee bits'í* ('man's body')
bijíí ('heart')	*bibiiye'* ('innards')	*ndee bits'í* ('man's body')
bijíí'izólé ('lung')	*bibiiye'* ('innards')	*ndee bits'í* ('man's body')

FIGURE 4. Taxonomic structure of anatomical set. (Note: Hatched areas indicate position in taxonomy of additional [i.e., unextended] anatomical terms.)

Set Extension

In dealing with the semantic extension of a single lexeme, the most that can be shown is that its associated category has been broadened to include a novel class of referents and, as a consequence, that the lexeme itself has acquired a new sense. At the level of the lexical set, however, it is apparent that extension involves more than the acquisition of new senses by individual lexemes. What is also involved, as we have seen, is an extension of classificatory principles and their structural interrelationships—in short, an entire taxonomic framework. Accordingly,

bi'ik'ah ('grease')		
biyedaa' ('front bumper')		
biwos ('front fender')		
bigan ('front wheel')		
bik'ai ('rear fender')		
bizé' ('gas pipe opening')		natbiil bits'í ('automobile's body')
bikee' ('rear wheel')		
bigháń ('bed of truck')		
bidáá' ('headlight')		
bichį́h ('hood')	binii'*	
bita' ('windshield')		
bits'ǫǫs ('electrical wiring')	bibiiye' ('all items under hood')	
bizig ('battery')		
bibid ('gas tank')		
bich'í' ('radiator hose')		
bijíí ('distributor')		
bijíí'izólé ('radiator')		

FIGURE 5. Taxonomic structure of extended set.
* 'area extending from top of windshield to front bumper'

set extension may be defined as the process in which all or part of a lexically coded taxonomy is mapped onto a portion of the environment that has not been previously classified.

The concept of set extension is a useful one. It allows us to generalize about semantic change at a level above the word by suggesting that entire lexical sets may be extended in a manner analogous to single lexemes. Extension of both sorts results in the expansion of existing semantic categories to include new referents. But set extension is unique in that it also entails the extension of intercategory relationships. If lexical sets and their associated conceptual domains are viewed as models of how speakers of a language construe the world around them, then set extension can be considered a process whereby old models are used to structure fresh experience.

A review of the literature on linguistic acculturation has uncovered only one other example of set extension.[1] This could be taken to mean that we are dealing with a very rare phenomenon, but more likely it indicates that linguists and ethnographers have not been in the habit of searching in the field for extended lexical sets. The additional example is provided by George Herzog (1941), who recorded a short list of Pima automobile terms—plainly anatomical extensions—that are similar in several respects to the Apache material discussed above. Unfortunately, the comparative utility of Herzog's corpus is limited on two counts. First, we cannot be sure that his list of extended Pima terms is complete, and second, the unextended meanings of the terms he presents are not precisely glossed. Nonetheless, it seems safe to conclude that the Western Apache were not alone in classifying the parts of motorized vehicles on the basis of an anatomical model. Indeed, the application of anatomical terms to motorized vehicles was probably for the Apache—and perhaps for the Pima as well—an ingenious adaptive move. Set extension facilitated communication about a totally foreign object in a familiar frame of reference and, at least for a while, made it unnecessary for Apaches to contend with an elaborate English terminology that even native speakers may sometimes find confusing.

A Semantic Explanation

In seeking to explain the extension of a lexical set we are not required to document the history of each of the set's constituent lexemes. Rather, we treat the set as a unit, assuming that an adequate explanation for its extension as a whole serves equally well for any and all of its members. But how should such an explanation be framed? More pointedly, how should we account for the fact that Western Apache anatomical terms were extended to automobiles and pickup trucks?

Let us begin by offering a functional explanation. Following their introduction by Anglo-Americans, motorized vehicles came to occupy a prominent place in the Western Apache transportation system that had formerly been filled by the horse; because anatomical terms were applied to horses, these terms were readily extended to their mechanized successors. On this account, set extension is explained as resulting from a functional equivalence between the category of objects customarily described by the extended set and the category of objects to which the set has been extended. I consider this explanation less than satisfactory. In the first place, too much depends on the putative correspondence of horse and car, a correspondence that several of my Apache consultants were eager to dispute. More important still, such an account is entirely removed from any aspect of language, thus implying (among a host of other misleading notions) that lexical changes cannot be profitably examined in relation to other linguistic phenomena.

An alternative explanation rests on the following assumption: when an item of foreign culture is incorporated into an established semantic category whose members are conventionally described with a particular lexical set, that set will be extended to cover the newly incorporated item. In this regard, it is interesting to note that motorized vehicles were classified by the Western Apache as instances of *'ihi'dahí*, a broad category that also includes humans, quadrupeds, birds, reptiles, fish, insects, plants, and several other engine-driven machines (e.g., bulldozers, tractors, steam shovels). This category contrasts with *destsǫǫhí*, which encompasses most topographical features and all but a few items of material culture. My investigation of these two categories has been fairly exhaustive, and it appears to be the case that *'ihi'dahí* includes only those phenomena that are capable of generating and sustaining their own movement. Conversely, *destsǫǫhí* is restricted to objects that are wholly immobile or depend for movement upon the action of external forces. So far as I have been able to determine, Apache anatomical terminologies are used exclusively in connection with members of the *'ihi'dahí* category. Members of the *destsǫǫhí* category are not described with anatomical sets, but with other nomenclatures that do not concern us here.

A semantic explanation may now be offered for the extension of Western Apache anatomical terms to motorized vehicles. When the automobile was first introduced, it was perceived by Apaches to possess a crucial defining attribute—the ability to move itself—and on this basis was incorporated into the *'ihi'dahí* category. The conventional practice of describing members of this category with anatomical terms was then applied to cars and pickup trucks, producing the extended set discussed above. That Model-T Fords were found by the Western Apache to possess "livers"—which were part of the vehicles' "innards," which in turn were part of their "bodies"—might well have been expected. It was, in a way, a matter of common sense.

3 / A Western Apache Writing System: The Symbols of Silas John

Co-authored by Ned Anderson

In a lengthy essay published in 1888–89, Garrick Mallery, a re-tired military officer employed as an anthropologist by the Bu-reau of American Ethnology, invited explorers, missionaries, and ethnographers to provide him with information pertaining to systems of graphic communication then in use among the Indian tribes of North America. Expressing his conviction that these "primitive forms of writing provide direct and significant evidence upon the evolution of an important aspect of human culture," Mallery also warned that they were rapidly disappear-ing, and that unless those in existence were studied immedi-ately the opportunity would be lost forever. Unfortunately for anthropology, Mallery's invitation went largely unheeded and his prophecy came true. In the closing decades of the nine-teenth century, a number of native graphic systems went out of existence and a fledgling social science, occupied with more ur-gent concerns, scarcely took note of their passing.

The lack of enthusiasm that greeted Mallery's early call for research set a precedent which was destined to continue, for to this day the ethnographic study of so-called primitive writing systems—including those stimulated by contact with Europe-ans—has failed to engage the sustained interests of either lin-guists or cultural anthropologists. The result, I. J. Gelb (1963 : 10) has observed, is that "Some of these writings are known very inadequately, others are known only from hearsay and still oth-ers must exist in obscure corners of the globe as yet unnoticed by scholars."[1]

Under these circumstances, it is with marked enthusiasm

that we greet the opportunity to report upon a previously un-described writing system which is in active use today among Western Apache Indians living on the Fort Apache and San Carlos reservations. This system has persisted essentially un-changed since its invention in 1904 by Silas John Edwards, a preeminent Western Apache shaman who was also the founder and leader of a nativistic religious movement which established itself on both Western Apache reservations in the early 1920s and subsequently spread to the Mescalero Apache in New Mexico.[2]

In 1971 Mr. Edwards was eighty-eight years old, almost blind, but still very much alive. Known to Apaches and Anglo-Americans alike simply as Silas John, he created a writing system so that an extensive set of prayers expressing the ideological core of his religion could be recorded in permanent form and dis-seminated among his followers. Although the content of these prayers is deeply influenced by Christian symbolism, a result of Silas John's early association with Lutheran missionaries on the Fort Apache reservation, the written script was entirely his own invention, initially conceived in a "dream from God" and later developed without assistance from Anglo-Americans or Apaches. An ability to read and write English, acquired by Silas John as a young man, undoubtedly accounts for his expo-sure to the idea of writing. However, it does not account for the graphic form of his script or its underlying structural principles, which depart radically from those of the English alphabet. Like the Cherokee syllabary invented by Sequoyah around 1820, the writing system of Silas John represents a classic case of stimu-lus diffusion that resulted in the creation of a totally unique cultural form. As such, we believe, it ranks among the signifi-cant intellectual achievements by an American Indian during the twentieth century.

Methodological Problems

Since Garrick Mallery's day and before, American Indian writ-ing systems have been described with a set of time-honored concepts that were originally devised by European epigraphers to classify distinct types of graphic symbols and, by extension, to classify whole systems. For example, if all the symbols in a particular system were identified as pictographs the system itself was classified *pictographic;* on the other hand, if stylized ideographs existed side by side with pictographs the system was termed *pictographic-ideographic.* In this way, different systems were compared on the basis of what types of symbols composed them and, in conjunction with historical data, arranged sequentially in order of their presumed chronological appearance.

The typologies constructed for these purposes, almost all of which classify graphs according to attributes of external form, are strictly etic in character, the products of a long tradition of Western scholarship that often lacked access to native consultants and was chiefly concerned with the formulation of broadscale comparative strategies.[3] Although no one would dispute the importance of such strategies or deny the fact that adequate typologies are basic to their development, it is essential to point out that serious problems may arise when etic concepts are applied a priori to the description of individual writing systems. Unless it is first established that the distinctions and contrasts imposed by these concepts coincide with those considered meaningful by users of the system, the resulting description is almost certain to suffer from bias and distortion. In the great majority of American Indian studies no such evidence is adduced.

The fact that the symbols in a writing system may be submitted to classification by some existing etic scheme should not be taken to mean that the classification is automatically, or even necessarily, relevant to an understanding of how the system works. It would be a simple task, for example, to classify every symbol in the Silas John script according to whether it is pictographic or ideographic. Yet, as we shall see, this distinction has no significance for the Western Apache, who classify these symbols on the basis of different criteria. An account of the Silas John script that ignored these native—or emic— distinctions, and proceeded instead in terms of the pictographic/ideographic contrast, would fail to reveal the basic principles that impart structure to the system as a whole. Simultaneously, and equally damaging, such an account would suggest that the system's operation was predicated on rules which, in fact, are irrelevant to it and altogether absent from Western Apache culture.

Methodological problems of this kind cannot be dismissed as inconsequential, nor can they be ignored on the supposition that their occurrence has been infrequent. To the contrary, a recent survey of the literature on American Indian graphic systems reveals the use of unverified etic concepts to be so pervasive that in all but a few cases it is impossible to determine the kinds of conceptual skills that were actually required to produce and interpret intelligible written messages.

The adequacy of an ethnographic description of a writing system should be judged by its ability to permit someone who is unfamiliar with the system—but who has a knowledge of the language on which it is based—to read and write. It should provide, in other words, an explicit formulation of the knowledge necessary to become literate. Among other things, this requires that the basic units in the system be identified and defined in accordance with criteria that persons already literate recognize as valid, necessary, and appropriate. If these criteria are not disclosed, or if they are arbitrarily replaced with criteria derived from the investigator's own culture, the knowledge necessary to use the system correctly will remain hidden.

Ward Goodenough (1970: 129) has observed that an adequate etic typology must be sufficiently sensitive "to describe all the emic distinctions people actually make in all the world's cultures in relation to the subject matter for which the etic concepts are designed." This requirement applies as much to typologies of writing as it does to those for any other cultural phenomena. Goodenough also emphasizes that the emic and etic enterprises are not mutually exclusive, but complementary and logically interrelated. Emic concepts provide us with what we need to know to construct valid etic concepts, while the latter, besides determining the form and content of comparative propositions, assist in the discovery and description of the former.

Studies of American Indian writing systems contain so few

emic analyses that the basic materials needed to construct adequate etic typologies are all but absent. Consequently, the few etic concepts that have been proposed are open to serious question. On the one hand, it has not been shown that these categories describe "all the emic distinctions people actually make"; on the other, they are so all-encompassing that their utility for comparative purposes is seriously impaired. Obviously, these difficulties cannot be overcome through the creation of more arbitrary categories. The surest solution lies in the continued investigation of individual writing systems which, if properly described, will contribute to an inventory of demonstrably relevant emic distinctions and thus assure that subsequent etic typologies have a more secure grounding in cultural fact. Our account of the Silas John writing system is intended as a contribution in this direction.

Development of the Writing System

In 1904, when Silas John Edwards was twenty-one years old and living in the community of East Fork on the Fort Apache Indian Reservation, he experienced a vision in which he was presented with a set of sixty-two prayers and an accompanying set of graphic symbols with which to write them. Silas John recalls his vision as follows:

> There were sixty-two prayers. They came to me in rays from above. At the same time I was instructed. He [God] was advising me and telling me what to do, at the same time teaching me chants. They were presented to me—one by one. All of these and the writing were given to me at one time in one dream. . . .

> God made it [the writing], but it came down to our earth. I liken this to what has happened in the religions we have now. In the center of the earth, when it first began, when the earth was first made, there was absolutely nothing on this world. There was no written language. So it was in 1904 that I became aware of the writing; it was then that I heard about it from God.

Silas John used his writing system for the sole purpose of recording the sixty-two prayers he received in his vision. The script was never applied to the large body of traditional Apache prayers already in existence by 1904, nor was it ever employed as a vehicle for secular speech. This is important to keep in mind because the merits of the script, as well as its limitations, stem directly from the fact that it was purposely designed to communicate information relevant to the performance of ritual and *not* to write the infinitude of messages capable of expression in spoken Western Apache.

In 1916, a full twelve years after Silas John experienced his vision, he publicly proclaimed himself a messiah and began to preach. At the same time, he wrote down each of his prayers on separate pieces of tanned buckskin, using paints made from a mixture of pulverized minerals and the sap of yucca plants. This technique of writing soon was replaced, however, and by 1925 prayer texts rendered in ink were appearing on squares of cardboard. Today, many (and possibly all) of the original painted buckskins have been lost or disposed of, and Silas John's script is preserved in paper 'prayer books' (*sailish jaan bi 'okąąhí*) belonging to Apaches living on the San Carlos and Fort Apache reservations.

By 1920, when it was apparent to Silas John that his acceptance as a religious prophet was assured, he selected twelve 'assistants' (*sailish jaan yiłnaanałseehí*) to circulate among the Apache people, pray for them, and encourage them to congregate. The assistants were given instruction in how to read and write and, after acquiring these skills, went through an initiation ritual in which they were presented with painted buckskins of their own. Thus equipped, they were placed in charge of carefully prepared sites known as 'holy grounds' and urged to perform ceremonials on a regular basis, using their buckskins as mnemonic aids. As time passed and members of the original group of assistants began to die, Silas John appointed new ones who in turn were taught the script, formally initiated, and given the texts of prayers. This process, which has continued unmodified up to the present, accounts for the fact that even among Apaches knowledge of Silas John's writing system is not widespread. From the very beginning, access to the system was tightly controlled by Silas John himself, and competence in it was initially restricted to a small band of elite ritual specialists. Commenting on this point, one of our Apache consultants observed:

> Silas John just let a few people know what the writing meant. He once told my father that it had to be kept just like it was when he heard about it from God. If some person ever tried to change it, he said, God would stop listening to the people when they prayed. He knew that if he let it out for all the people to know some wouldn't know about this, some wouldn't take it seriously. Maybe some would try to change it. So he just gave it to a few people, men and women who would learn it right—just the way he taught them—and leave it alone. It has been that way for a long time, and it [the writing] is still the way it was when it came to this earth from God.

Description of the Writing System

The following account of Silas John's writing system is based upon an analysis of six texts that were copied from a prayer book belonging to one of his youngest assistants on the San Carlos reservation. This was the only prayer book we were permitted to see, and although it contained several additional texts, instruction in these was prevented by the sudden and unexpected hospitalization of our chief consultant, a much older assistant whom Silas John had recommended as a particularly well-qualified teacher. The fact that we were unable to enlarge our sample hindered our analysis at certain points.[4] However, it did not prevent us from discovering the underlying principles according to which the writing system operates, the kind of information it conveys, or the concepts Apaches must learn to become literate. Our description should enable anyone with a knowledge of spoken Apache to read fully and correctly the six prayer texts that constitute our corpus. No more can honestly be claimed since these were the only texts in which we ourselves received adequate training and developed an acceptable measure of competence by Western Apache standards.

A 'Silas John prayer text' (*sailish jaan bi 'okąąhí*) may be defined as a set of graphic 'symbols' (*ke'eschín*) written on buckskin or paper whose members are arranged in horizontal lines

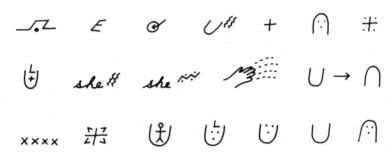

FIGURE 6. Text of 'prayer for life' in correct reading form, from left to right in descending order.

to be read from left to right in descending order (figure 6). Each symbol is separated from the one that follows it by an empty space and corresponds to a single line of prayer which may consist of a word, a phrase, or one or more sentences.

. The sixty-two prayers authored by Silas John are partitioned into three major categories: (1) 'prayers for life' (*bi'ihi'da' baa 'okąąhí*), which promote health, longevity, and the maintenance of tension-free social relations; (2) 'prayers for man and woman' (*ndee hik'e 'isdzán 'okąąhí*), which are invoked to combat and resolve marital discord; and (3) 'prayers for sickness' (*'ida'áń 'okąąhí*), which are employed to relieve physiological and mental illnesses caused by witchcraft, snakebite, or supernatural forces that have been antagonized by disrespectful behavior.

Prayers belonging to the same category are virtually identical in linguistic structure with the result that the number and sequential arrangement of their written symbols exhibit little variation. Consider, for example, the three 'prayers for life' whose texts are presented in figure 7; note that each text contains the same number of symbols (20) and that their serial order is disturbed at only two points (4 and 8). Because this kind of uniformity is typical, the texts in each prayer category manifest a characteristic pattern. Two of these patterns can be readily discerned by comparing the three texts of 'prayer for life' in figure 7 with the three texts of 'prayer for sickness' that appear in figure 8.

	TEXT 1	TEXT 2	TEXT 3
1			
2			
3			
4			
5			
6			
7			
8			
9			
10			
11			
12			
13			
14	x x x x	x x x x	x x x x
15			
16			
17			
18			
19	U	U	U
20			

FIGURE 7. Three texts of 'prayer for life', arranged in vertical order for ease of comparison.

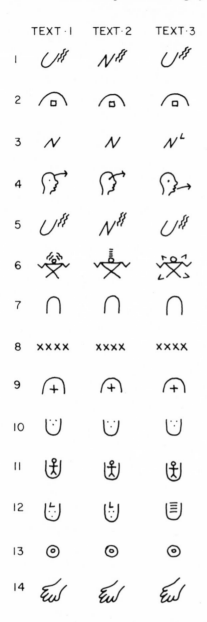

FIGURE 8. Three texts of 'prayer for sickness', arranged in vertical order for ease of comparison.

Western Apaches assert that symbols in the Silas John script are composed of isolable 'symbol elements' (also termed *ke'eschín*), and they emphasize that to write and read a prayer text properly it is essential to discriminate among symbols that consist of two or more elements and those that consist of only one. The former class, whose members we shall refer to as *compound symbols*, is labeled by the Western Apache expression *ke'eschín łeediidilgohí* ('symbol elements put together'), while the latter, whose members we shall refer to as *noncompound symbols*, is termed *ke'eschín doołeediidildahí* ('symbol elements standing alone'). Figure 9 presents the Apache classification of the symbols in our corpus into these two categories.

Symbol elements are not to be equated with discrete graphic components, for as a glance at figure 9 will show, noncompound symbols may consist of more than one component. For example, the symbol ⊘ , which might suggest itself to an outsider as having two graphic components— ○ and ↙ —is not construed as such by Apaches, who consider it a noncompound symbol that cannot be dissected. The reason, our consultants explained, is that by themselves neither ○ nor ↙ has meaning and, as a result, must always occur in association with each other. In other words, they become semantically viable only as a unit, and in this respect contrast sharply with the components of compound symbols which, besides having meaning in combination, also have meaning in isolation. Thus we arrive at an important insight: the classification of compound and noncompound symbols is based upon other than visual criteria and cannot be deduced solely from the inspection of a symbol's outer form.

When requested to identify and define the individual symbol elements in our corpus, our consultants sorted them into three classes. One class (A) is made up of elements that only occur in isolation and function exclusively in the capacity of noncompound symbols. Elements in the second class (B) also occur alone, but in addition can be combined with other elements to form compound symbols. The third class (C) consists of elements that occur only in compound symbols and never in isolation. In figure 10 each of the twenty-eight symbol elements

NON-COMPOUND SYMBOLS		COMPOUND SYMBOLS	
1		1	
2	E	2	
3		3	
4		4	
5	x x x x	5	
6		6	
7		7	
8		8	
9		9	
10		10	
11		11	
12		12	
13		13	
14	U	14	
15	N	15	
16	+	16	she
17	∩	17	she
		18	
		19	

FIGURE 9. Noncompound and compound symbols.

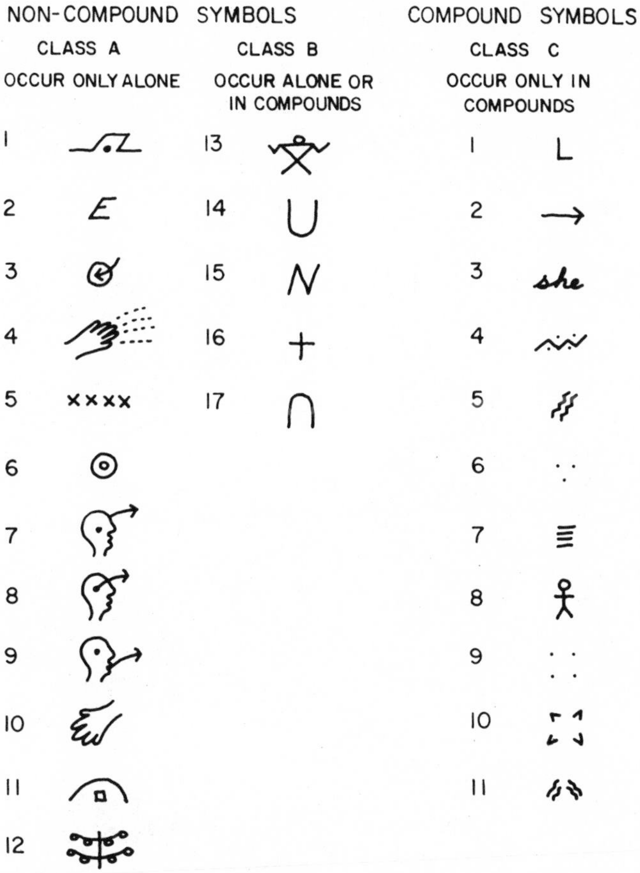

FIGURE 10. Symbols grouped into classes A, B, and C.

that appear in our corpus has been assigned to one of these three classes.

Compound symbols may be divided into five structural types according to the number of elements they contain (two or three) and the classes (B and/or C) to which these elements belong. For the sake of convenience and economy, the members of each type are expressed in figure 11 as the outcome of simple formulas that operate on individual elements and specify the manner in which they are combined. We make no claim for the psy-

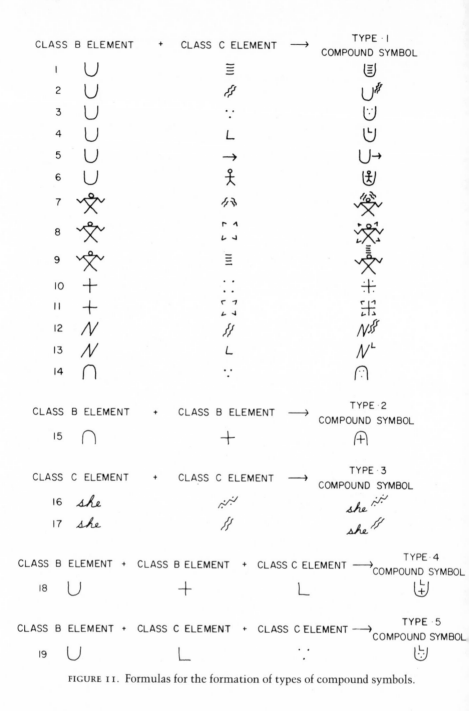

FIGURE 11. Formulas for the formation of types of compound symbols.

chological reality of either the typology or the formulas; they are employed here simply as descriptive devices that allow us to make formally explicit the knowledge an Apache must possess in order to form the compound symbols that appear in the prayer texts at our disposal.

COMPOUND SYMBOL TYPE 1: one element from class B is combined with one element from class C.

COMPOUND SYMBOL TYPE 2: one element from class B is combined with one other element from class B.

COMPOUND SYMBOL TYPE 3: one element from class C is combined with one other element from class C.

COMPOUND SYMBOL TYPE 4: two elements from class B are combined with one element from class C.

COMPOUND SYMBOL TYPE 5: one element from class B is combined with two elements from class C.

A striking feature of the Silas John script is that it encodes information relevant to the production of nonverbal behavior as well as speech. This is made explicit in a distinction Apaches draw between 'symbols that tell what to say' (*ke'eschín hant'é ndíí*) and 'symbols that tell what to do' (*ke'eschín hant'é 'aile'*). All symbols 'tell what to say' in the sense that each one signals the vocalization of some particular prayer line. However, a few symbols—those that 'tell what to do'—function simultaneously to signal the performance of key ritual actions without which the prayer, no matter how correct in its linguistic details, is considered incomplete.

In essence, then, a prayer text consists of a set of highly detailed instructions that specify what an individual must say and do to perform ceremonials in a manner that satisfies the standards held by Silas John and the members of his religion. So fundamental is the knowledge necessary to read these instructions, Apaches claim, that any attempt to execute the role of 'ceremonial leader' (*diiyin*) without it is certain to be flawed and unacceptable. One of our consultants commented on this as follows:

> It's all in here [pointing to a prayer text], how to pray in just the right way. That's why he [Silas John] made them like this, so

the ones who pray can be sure they know how to do it right. Only the ones who can read can pray. . . . I heard of a man at Whiteriver who wanted to be a ceremonial leader like the ones who work for Silas John. So he went to many ceremonials and tried to watch everything they did. After a long time he thought he knew what to do and got ready to try it out. . . . The people came to where he was and he started up. But pretty soon they knew he didn't really know it. . . . This was because no one had taught him to read buckskins; he couldn't do it without them. When he [Silas John] chooses you to be a ceremonial leader, first you learn what the symbols say, then, after that, what the symbols mean for you to do. You must know both because if you don't you will make mistakes like that Whiteriver man I was telling you about before.

Meaning of the Symbols

The process of learning what the symbols in a prayer text represent may be considered complete when the linguistic referent of each symbol—that is, the prayer line it serves to recall in the performance of a ceremonial—has been committed to memory. The process begins, however, with the memorization of expressions that define the meaning of symbol elements. These expressions are termed 'symbol elements names' (*ke'eschín bízhi'*) and are held by Apaches to constitute the basic semantic units of the Silas John writing system.

The 'names' of elements that function as noncompound symbols are identical to the prayer lines these symbols elicit in ritual contexts. Consequently, the linguistic referent of a noncompound symbol is always isomorphic with the meaning of the element that forms it and can be learned in a single operation. The linguistic referents of the noncompound symbols that appear in our corpus (those symbols formed by elements in class A and, when occurring in isolation, elements in class B) are presented below. The numbers refer to the symbols in figure 10.

Noncompound Symbols

CLASS A ELEMENTS (occur only alone)

1. ni'gosdzáń 'áwolzggng': 'earth, when it was made'
2. yaa' 'áwolzggng': 'sky, when it was made'
3. da'iłtséh dagoyggng' ni'gosdzáń 'iłdjjzhé': 'first, when it all began in the center of the earth'
4. shilagan hadaazhé' djjgo bihadaa'istjjgo: 'my fingers, from their tips, like four rays, power emanates'
   shilagan hadaazhé djjgo bihadit'jjgo: 'my fingers, from their tips, power illuminates all'[5]
5. naago'ááhí naagoschǫhí naagołdííhí beehegoz'íní: 'sinful things occurring, bad things occurring, sickness and evil occurring, together with harmful knowledge'[6]
6. bijíí hádndín: 'his heart, sacred pollen'
7. ya'itsii 'akoshyó: 'from where his thoughts dwell'
8. ya'odishyó: 'from where he looks out'
9. ya'iiyałti'yó: 'from where he speaks out'
10. yóósn bi'ihi'dááhí binaadidzooł beehe'ndzílí yéédaadoldí tsiyaago daadoldí' nikǫ'zhę': 'with his life, his breath, his power, God extends his hand and blesses you'
11. yóósn bi gowǫ: 'God, his dwelling'
12. hádndín ła'ashníídn: 'he who is decorated with and enriched by much pollen'[7]

CLASS B ELEMENTS (occur alone or in compounds)

13. hádndín 'ishkiin: 'sacred pollen boy'[8]
14. yóósn: 'God'
15. nayééneezgháné: 'Jesus'
16. hádndín 'iłna'áhí: 'sacred pollen, that which is crossed'
17. ni'gosdzáń bika' latáázhé': 'world, on the surface of it'

The 'names' of elements in class C must also be memorized since a knowledge of these constructions, together with those that label class B elements, is basic to the interpretation of compound symbols. The numbers refer to the symbols in figure 10.

CLASS C ELEMENTS (occur only in compounds)

1. 'ihi'da: 'life'
2. 'intin: 'path', 'trail', 'road'

3. *shíí:* 'I', 'me', 'mine'
4. *'okąąhí:* 'prayer, that which is'
5. *hádndín:* 'sacred pollen'
6. *hádndín:* 'sacred pollen'
7. *hádndín:* 'sacred pollen'
8. *ndee* 'man', 'men'[9]
9. *dííyó:* 'four places'
10. *díízhę':* 'in', or 'from four directions'
11. *díídń:* 'four times'

When an Apache learns the expressions that label elements in a compound symbol, he or she does not simultaneously learn that symbol's associated prayer line. This is because the linguistic referents of compound symbols are never isomorphic with the 'names' of the class B and/or C elements that form them. Consider, for example, compound symbol 2 (figure 11). The meaning of class B element 14 is *yóósn* ('God',) and the meaning of class C element 5 (Figure 10) is *hádndín* ('sacred pollen'). The prayer line evoked by compound symbol 2 is *yóósn bi hádndín* ('God, his sacred pollen') which, while replicating exactly the meanings of its elements, is not identical to either one because of the addition of the possessive pronoun *bi* ('his'). It should be emphasized that the degree of correspondence between the referent of a compound symbol and the expressions that define its elements is not always this high. In the case of compound symbol 5 (figure 11), for example, whose referent is *dashizhǫǫ bee'ishgaał ch'indii* ('it is said that I alone go forth with this power'), the meaning of class B element 14 (figure 10) is *yóósn* ('God') and that of class C element 2 is *'intin* ('path', 'trail', 'road').

Because the prayer line associated with a compound symbol is structurally and semantically more complex than the 'names' of its elements, it cannot be inferred from them and, as a consequence, must be memorized separately. However, since the 'names' either form some part of the prayer line or allude metaphorically to key concepts embedded within it, the elements serve as indispensable aids for bringing the prayer line to mind.

The linguistic referents of the compound symbols in our cor-

pus are as follows. The numbers refer to the symbols in figures
10 and 11.

COMPOUND SYMBOL TYPE I

1. Class B element 14 (*yóósn:* 'God') plus class C element 7
(*hádndín:* 'pollen') produces compound symbol 1 (*yóósn bi
hádndín:* 'God, his sacred pollen')¹⁰
2. Class B element 14 (*yóósn:* 'God') plus class C element 5
(*hádndín:* 'pollen') produces compound symbol 2 (*yóósn bi
hádndín:* 'God, his sacred pollen')
3. Class B element 14 (*yóósn:* 'God') plus class C element 6
(*hádndín:* 'pollen') produces compound symbol 3 (*yóósn bi
hádndín:* 'God, his sacred pollen')
4. Class B element 14 (*yóósn:* 'God') plus class C element 1
(*'ihi'da:* 'life') produces compound symbol 4 (*yóósn bi'ihi'da:*
'God, his life')
5. Class B element 14 (*yóósn:* 'God') plus class C element 2
(*'intin:* 'path', 'trail', 'road') produces compound symbol 5
(*dashízhǫǫ bee'ishgaał ch'indii:* 'it is said that I alone go forth
with this power')
6. Class B element 14 (*yóósn:* 'God') plus class C element 8
(*ndee:* 'man', 'men') produces compound symbol 6 (*bitł'áh
nabąązhę' yóósn biyi' sizįįhí:* 'following this, God entered
into man')
7. Class B element 13 (*hádndín 'ishkiin:* 'sacred pollen
boy') plus class C element 11 (*dįįdń:* 'four times') produces
compound symbol 7 (*dįįdń hádndín 'ishkinihí:* 'four times,
that which is sacred pollen boy')
8. Class B element 13 (*hádndín 'ishkiin:* 'sacred pollen
boy') plus class C element 10 (*dįįzhę':* 'from four directions')
produces compound symbol 8 (*hádndín 'iskhiin dįįzhę' nadi-
yołhí:* 'sacred pollen boy, he who breathes in four directions')
9. Class B element 13 (*hádndín 'ishkiin:* 'sacred pollen
boy') plus class C element 7 (*hádndín:* 'sacred pollen') produces compound symbol 9 (*'iziidahsidil hádndín 'ishkiin:*
'from above it cures, pollen boy')
10. Class B element 16 (*hádndín iłna'áhí:* 'sacred pollen,

that which is crossed') plus class C element 9 (*dįįyó:* 'four places') produces compound symbol 10 (*hádndín iłna'áhí dįįyó nadiyoł:* 'sacred pollen, that which is crossed, breathing in four places')

11. Class B element 16 (*hádndín iłna'áhí:* 'sacred pollen, that which is crossed') plus class C element 10 (*dįįzhę':* 'in four directions') produces compound symbol 11 (*dįįzhę' biłhadaagoyaa:* 'these things dispersed in four directions')

12. Class B element 15 (*nayééneezghání:* 'Jesus') plus class C element 5 (*hádndín:* 'sacred pollen') produces compound symbol 12 (*nayééneezghání bi hádndín:* 'Jesus, his sacred pollen')

13. Class B element 15 (*nayééneezghání:* 'Jesus') plus class C element 1 (*'ihi'da':* 'life') produces compound symbol 13 (*nayééneezghání bi'ihi'da':* 'Jesus, his life')

14. Class B element 17 (*ni'gosdzáń:* 'world') plus class C element 6 (*hádndín:* 'sacred pollen') produces compound symbol 14 (*hádndín 'ihi'dahí:* 'sacred pollen, that which is alive')[11]

COMPOUND SYMBOL TYPE 2

15. Class B element 17 (*ni'gosdzáń:* 'world') plus class B element 16 (*hádndín iłna'áhí:* 'sacred pollen, that which is crossed') produces compound symbol 15 (*hádndín iłna'áhí ni'gosdzáń bikázhę':* 'pollen, that which is crossed, on the surface of the world')

COMPOUND SYMBOL TYPE 3

16. Class C element 3 (*shíí:* 'I', 'me', 'mine') plus class C element 4 (*'okąąhí:* 'prayer') produces compound symbol 16 (*shíí 'okąąhí:* 'mine, that which is my prayer')

17. Class C element 3 (*shíí:* 'I', 'me', 'mine') plus class C element 5 (*hádndín:* 'sacred pollen') produces compound symbol 17 (*shíí shi hádndínihí:* 'mine, that which is my sacred pollen')

COMPOUND SYMBOL TYPE 4

18. Class B element 14 (*yóósn:* 'God') plus class B element 16 (*hádndín iłna'áhí:* 'sacred pollen, that which is crossed')

plus class C element 1 (*'ihi'da:* 'life') produces compound symbol 18 (*yóósn bi hádndín iłna'áhí 'ihi'dahí:* 'God, his sacred pollen, that which is crossed, that which is alive')

COMPOUND SYMBOL TYPE 5

19. Class B element 14 (*yóósn:* 'God') plus class C element 6 (*hádndín:* 'sacred pollen') plus class C element 1 (*'ihi'da:* 'life') produces compound symbol 19 (*yóósn binaadidzoołhí:* 'God, that which is his breath')[12]

Coding of Nonverbal Behavior

We have already drawn attention to the fact that certain symbols in the Silas John script call for the performance of specific types of nonverbal behavior as well as the utterance of a prayer line. To cite an example, compound symbol 2 (figure 11) requires that simultaneous with the vocalization of its linguistic referent, which is *yóósn bi hádndín* ('God, his sacred pollen'), the speaker bless the ritual paraphernalia that identify him as a ceremonial leader by sprinkling each item with a pinch of cattail pollen. Actions of this kind, which constitute what we shall henceforth describe as a symbol's *kinetic* referent, consistently involve the manipulation of material culture, and for this reason a brief description of the physical settings in which ceremonials take place is essential.

All rituals connected with the Silas John religion are conducted within the perimeters of what both monolingual and bilingual Apaches call 'holy grounds'. These are small areas of land, usually about 15 feet square, whose corners correspond to the four cardinal directions and are marked by upright wooden crosses (*'iłna'áhí ndeez:* 'long crosses'). Each cross is approximately 7 feet tall, painted a different color—black (east), yellow (north), green (west), and white (south)—and decorated with the breast feathers of eagles.

Other objects of material culture that assume importance in ceremonial activities include:

1. 'wooden hoops' (*bą́ą́sé*). Used only in rituals held for the purpose of curing the sick, hoops are made in sets of four

and suspended on the crosses that define the corners of 'holy grounds'. Each hoop is roughly a yard in diameter, painted to match the color of the cross on which it hangs, and adorned with eagle feathers or strips of colored ribbon.

2. 'painted buckskins' (*'iban ke'eschín*). Every ceremonial leader is the owner of one or more buckskins which he or she spreads on the ground before the start of a ceremonial. Roughly square or rectangular, these buckskins are inscribed with non-orthographic symbols that represent 'sand paintings' (*ni' kegos-chii'*), and unless the ceremonial is of a particular type that requires the creation of these designs, the buckskins serve no mnemonic purpose.

3. 'personal crosses' (*ndee bi 'iłna'áhí*). Every ceremonial leader also owns a personal cross, which he or she displays at ritual gatherings by placing it on top of his or her buckskins. From 10 to 14 inches long and 6 to 10 inches wide, these objects are fashioned from wood and are sometimes enclosed in an outer covering of buckskin. An eagle feather and at least one turquoise bead are attached to the center of personal crosses with a strand of sinew, and it is not unusual to see specimens whose arms have been painted yellow.

4. 'sacred pollen' (*hádndín*). All ceremonials involve the use of cattail pollen, which is kept in an open container (usually a shallow basket) that is placed on the ground near the ceremonial leader's buckskins and personal cross.

We may now return to our prayer texts and discuss in greater detail 'symbols that tell what to do'. Ten symbols of this type occur in our corpus. Each is a compound symbol and is listed below with a description of the actions that collectively comprise its kinetic referent. In keeping with the verbal style of our Apache consultants, these descriptions are phrased as instructions to be followed by ceremonial leaders.

    1. Compound symbol 17—Face toward the east. Extend fully the right arm, fold the left arm across the chest, and bow the head. After remaining in this position for a few moments, drop the left arm and trace the sign of a cross on one's chest.

    2. Compound symbol 1—Face toward the east. Take a

pinch of sacred pollen in the right hand and hold it directly over the ritual paraphernalia, which are lying on the ground.

3. Compound symbol 3—Take a pinch of sacred pollen in the right hand and trace four circles in the air directly over the ritual paraphernalia.

4. Compound symbol 2—Take a pinch of sacred pollen in the right hand and place a small amount on each item of ritual paraphernalia.

5. Compound symbol 12—Same as number 4.

6. Compound symbol 10—Take a pinch of sacred pollen in the right hand and place a small amount on each arm of the ceremonial cross that marks the eastern corner of the holy ground.

7. Compound symbol 11—Same as number 6.

8. Compound symbol 9—Take a pinch of sacred pollen in the right hand and place a small amount on the head of the person (seated on the ground) for whom the ceremonial is being given.

9. Compound symbol 8—Take a pinch of sacred pollen in the right hand and with the same hand trace the sign of a cross on the chest of the person for whom the ceremonial is being given.

10. Compound symbol 7—Remove the wooden hoop from the cross that defines the eastern corner of the holy ground and pass it four times over the head and shoulders of the person for whom the ceremonial is being given.

'Symbols that tell what to do' appear to be the only ones in the Silas John script that sometimes lack unique linguistic referents. We have seen, for example, that the referent of compound symbol 1 (*yóósn bi hádndín:* 'God, his sacred pollen') is identical to that of compound symbols 2 and 3. Nor is it the case that all symbols of this type possess unique kinetic referents; the actions associated with compound symbol 10 are exactly the same as those associated with compound symbol 11. It should be noted, however, that symbols with identical linguistic referents never possess the same kinetic referents, and vice versa. In other words, two symbols may be kinetic allographs or they may be linguistic allographs, but they are never both at once and consequently complete redundancy is avoided.

According to one of our consultants, the kinetic values of 'symbols that tell what to do' are indirectly expressed by their linguistic referents. In some instances, this seems plausible, as when compound symbol 17 (*shíí shi hádndínihí:* 'mine, that which is my sacred pollen') calls for the ceremonial leader to bless himself or herself with cattail pollen. However, in other cases, the relationship is more obscure, as with compound symbol 2 (*yóósn bi hádndín:* 'God, his sacred pollen'), which requires the ceremonial leader to perform a blessing on his or her ritual paraphernalia.

What is significant is not that symbols vary in the extent to which their kinetic values can be inferred from their linguistic referents, but rather that they encode both types of information. Silas John might easily have chosen to convey kinetic instructions with one set of symbols and linguistic instructions with another. Instead, he created a script in which single symbols function in both capacities, thereby reducing the total number of symbols in the system and endowing it with added economy.

It should now be possible for the reader to translate into speech and action any and all of the prayer texts in our corpus. At this stage, of course, he or she will not have memorized the referent(s) of every symbol element and therefore will not be able to read spontaneously. However, a complete inventory of these referents has been provided as well as an explicit formulation of the rules that govern their combination and interpretation.

In general terms, the reader of a prayer text must be able to distinguish compound symbols from noncompound symbols, associate each with a particular linguistic construction, and pronounce that construction in Western Apache. In addition, he or she must be able to recognize symbols that call for nonverbal behavior, assign to each of these a particular kinetic referent, and transform that referent into the appropriate set of ritual gestures. With these skills and an ability to apply them swiftly and flawlessly in the physical context of a 'holy ground', our newly literate reader should be able to give a total performance that comes satisfactorily close to those expected of experienced Apache ceremonial leaders.

Translation of 'Prayer for Life'

As an illustration of what these performances consist of, we now present a detailed account of the 'prayer for life' that appears in figure 6. The Apache text is accompanied by full kinetic instructions and a free translation of the linguistic material which attempts to capture some of the drama and dignity of Silas John's ritual poetry. Numbers refer to symbols in text 1, figure 7.

1. *ni'gosdzáń 'áwolzᶐᶐnᶐ':* 'when the earth was first created'

2. *yaa' 'áwolzᶐᶐnᶐ':* 'when the sky was first created'

3. *da'iłtsé dágoyᶐᶐnᶐ ni'gosdzáń 'iłdíízhᶒ':* 'in the beginning, when all was started in the center of the earth'

4. *yóósn bi hádndín:* 'God's sacred pollen' (Take a pinch of sacred pollen in the right hand and place a small amount on each item of ritual paraphernalia.)

5. *hádndín 'iłna'áhí:* 'a cross of sacred pollen'

6. *hádndín 'ihi'dahí:* 'living sacred pollen'

7. *hádndín 'iłna'áhí dííyó nadiyoł:* 'a cross of sacred pollen breathing in four directions' (Take a pinch of sacred pollen in the right hand and place a small amount on each arm of the ceremonial cross that marks the eastern corner of the holy ground.)

8. *yóósn bi hádndín 'iłna'áhí 'ihi'dahí:* 'God's cross of living sacred pollen'

9. *shíí shi hádndínihí:* 'my own, my sacred pollen' (Face towards the east, extend fully the right arm, fold the left arm across the chest, and bow the head. After remaining in this position for a few moments, drop the left arm and trace the sign of a cross on one's chest.)

10. *shíí shi 'okᶐᶐhí:* 'my own, my prayer'

11. *shilagan hadᶐᶐzhᶒ' díígo bihadaa'istíígo:* 'like four rays, power is flowing forth from the tips of my fingers'

shilagan hadǫǫzhę' bihadit'įįgo: 'power from the tips of my fingers brings forth light'

12. *daashizhǫǫ bee'ishghaał ch'indii:* 'now it is known that I go forth with power'

13. *ni'gosdzáń bighaltaazhę':* 'on the surface of the world'

14. *naago'ááhí naagoschǫhí naagołdííhí beehegoz'íní:* 'sinful things are occurring, bad things are occurring, sickness and evil are occurring, together with harmful knowledge'

15. *díízhę' bił hadaagoyaa:* 'in four directions, these things are dispersed and fade away' (Take a pinch of sacred pollen in the right hand and place a small amount on each arm of the cross that marks the eastern corner of the holy ground.)

16. *bitł'áh nabǫǫzhę':* 'following this, God came to live with man'

17. *yóósn bi naadidzoołhí:* 'the breath of God'

18. *yóósn bi hádndín:* 'God's sacred pollen' (Take a pinch of sacred pollen in the right hand and trace four circles in the air directly over the ritual paraphernalia.)

19. *yóósn:* 'God Himself'

20. *hádndín 'ihi'dahí:* 'living sacred pollen'

Summary and Conclusion

At the outset of this essay we observed that the adequacy of an etic typology of written symbols could be judged by its ability to describe all the emic distinctions in all the writing systems of the world. In conclusion, we should like to return to this point and briefly examine the extent to which presently available etic concepts can be used to describe the distinctions made by Western Apaches in relation to the writing system of Silas John.

Every symbol in the Silas John script may be classified as a *phonetic semantic sign.* Symbols of this type denote linguistic expressions that consist of one or more words and contrast as a class with *phonetic nonsemantic signs,* which denote phonemes (or phoneme clusters), syllables (or syllable clusters), and various prosodic phenomena.

Phonetic semantic signs are commonly partitioned into two subclasses: *logographs,* which denote single words, and *phraseo-*

graphs, which denote multilexemic constructions. Although every symbol in the Silas John script can be assigned to one or the other of these categories, such an exercise is without justification. We have no evidence to suggest that Apaches classify symbols according to the length or complexity of their linguistic referents, and therefore the imposition of distinctions based on these criteria would be inappropriate, irrelevant, and misleading.

A far more useful contrast, and one we have already employed, is presented in most etic typologies as an opposition between *compound* (or composite) and *noncompound* (or noncomposite) symbols. Used to partition the category of phonetic semantic signs, these two concepts enable us to describe more or less exactly the distinction Apaches draw between 'symbol elements put together' (*ke'eschín łeediidilgohí*) and 'symbol elements standing alone (*ke'eschín doołeediidildahí*). The former may be defined as consisting of *compound phonetic semantic signs,* while the latter is composed of *noncompound phonetic semantic signs.*

Up to this point etic concepts have served us well. However, a deficiency appears when we search for a terminology that allows us to describe the distinction between 'symbols that tell what to say' (*ke'eschín hant'é ndíí*) and 'symbols that tell what to do' (*ke'eschín hant'é 'aile'*). As far as we have been able to determine, standard typologies make no provision for this kind of contrast, apparently because their creators have tacitly assumed that systems composed of phonetic semantic signs serve exclusively to communicate linguistic information. Consequently, the possibility that these systems might also convey nonlinguistic information seems to have been consistently ignored. This oversight may be a product of Western ethnocentrism; after all, it is we who use alphabets who most frequently associate writing with language. On the other hand, it may simply stem from the fact that systems incorporating symbols with kinetic referents are exceedingly rare and have not yet been reported. In any case, it is important to recognize that the etic inventory is incomplete.

Retaining the term *phonetic sign* as a label for written symbols that denote linguistic phenomena, we propose that the term *kinetic sign* be introduced to label symbols that denote sequences of nonverbal behavior. Symbols of the latter type that simultaneously denote some unit of language may be classified as *phonetic-kinetic* signs. With these concepts the contrast between 'symbols that tell what to say' and 'symbols that tell what to do' can be rephrased as one that distinguishes phonetic signs (by definition nonkinetic) from phonetic-kinetic signs. Pure kinetic signs—symbols that refer solely to physical gestures—are absent from the Silas John script.

The utility of kinetic sign and phonetic-kinetic sign as comparative concepts must ultimately be judged on the basis of their capacity to clarify and describe emic distinctions in other systems of writing. However, as we have previously pointed out, ethnographic studies of American Indian systems that address themselves to the identification of these distinctions—and thus provide the information necessary to evaluate the relevance and applicability of etic concepts—are in short supply. As a result, meaningful comparisons cannot be made. At this point, we simply lack the data with which to determine whether the kinetic component so prominent in the Silas John script is unique or whether it had counterparts elsewhere in North America.

The view is still prevalent among anthropologists and linguists that the great majority of American Indian writing systems conform to one or two global "primitive" types. Our study of the Silas John script casts doubt upon this position, for it demonstrates that fundamental emic distinctions remain to be discovered, and that existing etic frameworks are less than adequately equipped to describe them. The implications of these findings are clear. On the one hand, we must acknowledge the possibility that several structurally distinct forms of writing were developed by North America's Indian cultures. Concomitantly, we must be prepared to abandon traditional ideas of typological similarity and simplicity among these systems in favor of those that take variation and complexity into fuller account.

4 / 'Wise Words' of the Western Apache: Metaphor and Semantic Theory

The greatest thing by far is to be a master of metaphor. It is the one thing that cannot be learnt from others; and it is also a sign of genius, since a good metaphor implies an intuitive perception of the similarity in dissimilars.

ARISTOTLE

Introduction

The subject of metaphor, wrote Michel Bréal, is inexhaustible (1964:127). And so it would seem, for ever since the fourth century B.C., when Aristotle expressed his opinion that metaphor was the highest form of verbal art, this subtle instrument of language has been the object of serious thought and, in certain quarters, a source of richly informative debate. Yet, as Clifford Geertz (1964:58) points out, despite the accomplishments of this venerable tradition of inquiry—a tradition, it should be added, which now boasts an enormous body of literature and embraces disciplines as diverse as philosophy, rhetoric, and literary criticism—the study of metaphor remains marginal to the major concerns of most social scientists. This lack of interest is both ironic and regrettable because today, perhaps more than at any time in the past, anthropologists and linguists are in a position to construct theoretical models that can contribute in useful ways to a clearer understanding of the semantics of metaphor and the role of metaphor in cultural systems.

I assume that an adequate theory of metaphor must articulate with a theory of language—and by direct implication a theory of linguistic competence—that satisfactorily explains the ability of human beings to produce and interpret figurative speech. Such a theory has not yet been formulated within the paradigm of transformational linguistics nor does its development there seem probable. This is because the goals of modern semantics have been defined in such a way that a transformational grammar need only make explicit the tacit knowledge that enables the speaker of a language to assign literal or propositional meanings to sentence types. If such a grammar is taken to constitute a finished theory of language, as well as a complete model of the linguistic competence of its speakers, it is possible to conclude that the knowledge necessary to assign figurative meanings to sentences is "nonlinguistic" and that the ability to implement this knowledge lies outside the sphere of competence. This is what a number of transformationalists have claimed or implied, and in so doing they have exempted themselves—and their theory—from having to explain the fact that many sentences in a language can be, are, and in some instances *must* be interpreted in ways that are not predictable from an understanding of their literal meanings alone.

Simultaneously, an image has been created of man as "ideal speaker-hearer" (Chomsky 1965:3) which from an anthropological perspective is not ideal at all. Indeed, it is quite disturbing. For the ideal speaker-hearer as depicted by transformational grammarians is a person ("machine" is clearly a more accurate term) whose linguistic competence does not allow him to make meaningful sense of metaphorical speech. This hypothetical individual, we are informed, knows his language perfectly. Yet this same knowledge, complete, unflawed, and impeccable as it purportedly is, presents him with no alternative but to interpret a sentence such as "Cops are pigs" as a piece of poppycock arising from a confusion of policemen with a class of barnyard animals. It stands to reason that as long as this image of the ideal speaker-hearer persists unmodified, and as long as linguistic competence is restricted exclusively to the kinds of information contained in transformational grammars, attempts to construct an adequate theory of metaphor will be severely hampered.

One possible solution to this problem is to enlarge the concept of competence to include the full complement of skills and abilities that permit the members of a speech community to assign nonliteral meanings to spoken and written messages. But what are these skills and abilities? And how are they to be discovered? This much seems clear. The knowledge required to interpret metaphor in a culturally appropriate manner cannot be prescribed a priori. Rather, it must be inferred on the basis of detailed investigations of how actual instances of metaphor are constructed and construed. Initially, we must go about our business empirically, determining for particular societies what kinds of statements count as metaphors, what kinds of statements count as interpretations or "explanatory paraphrases" (Urban 1939 : 39) of metaphors, and perhaps most important of all, what kinds of standards are invoked to define some interpretations as more appropriate than others. In short, we must follow Dell Hymes's (1964, 1971) suggestion and do "ethnographies of speech," in this case, ethnographies of metaphorical speech.

In this essay I shall outline a model for the analysis of metaphor and apply it to a small body of metaphorical statements made by residents of Cibecue. Concomitantly, I will attempt to make more explicit what Aristotle and others have implied, namely that the production and interpretation of metaphorical speech involves a genuinely *creative* skill. Proceeding on the assumption that the successful interpretation of any metaphor entails the formation of at least one unitary concept, I will present evidence which suggests that these concepts are not lexically coded in the Western Apache language. On the basis of this discovery, I shall go on to argue that the interpretation of metaphor is grounded in an ability to form *novel semantic categories*. Such an ability is not accounted for by the standard transformational model of language, and I will conclude by discussing the implications of this deficiency for the revision of key linguistic concepts and the construction of an adequate theory of metaphor.

Metaphor as Simile

The most salient characteristic of metaphor consists in an apparent violation of linguistic rules that results in the expression of a proposition that is either logically false or, in Rudolf Carnap's (1955 : 47) terminology, "conceptually absurd." Walker Percy (1958 : 81) has put the matter nicely: a metaphor "asserts of one thing that it is something else" and is therefore inevitably "wrong." At the same time, of course, a metaphor is also "right" because, semantic disobedience notwithstanding, the proposition it expresses can be construed as containing a truth. Interpreted one way, Thomas Brown's metaphor, "Oh blackbird, what a boy you are," is utter nonsense since it is simply not the case that blackbirds are boys, or vice versa. On the other hand, this statement can be taken to mean that despite numerous differences there is some sense in which boys and blackbirds are alike—in their penchant for loud noise, for example, or in their propensity for energetic play. Herein lies a dilemma: how is it that a metaphorical statement can be at once both true and false?

This question is most commonly answered by asserting that metaphor is simile in disguise, a view which rests upon the more basic claim that an analytic distinction can be drawn between semantic features that compose the *designative* or *literal* meanings of words and features that compose their *connotative* or *figurative* meanings. Designative features are relatively few in number and serve as a set to specify the necessary and sufficient conditions for membership in the class of objects referred to by the word in question. Connotative features are much more numerous, are nondefining in the sense just described, and consist of any and all "associated commonplaces" (Black 1962:32) or "contingent facts" (Katz 1972:285) which the designative meaning(s) of the word call(s) to mind.

If designative meanings are relied upon to interpret a metaphor, the reasoning goes, the proposition it expresses will be understood as false or, at worst, contradictory. However, if the metaphor is construed as a covert simile, it will be understood as expressing a noncontradictory proposition whose truth value can be assessed—and, for those in a position to do so, established—on the basis of connotative meanings. The trick to interpreting a metaphor, then, is to reject it as a declarative proposition (e.g., Blackbirds are boys), interpret it as a comparative proposition (e.g., Blackbirds are *like* boys), and confirm the truth of the latter by adducing at least one valid similarity between the classes of objects being compared (e.g., Blackbirds are like boys *by virtue of* a shared fondness for whooping it up).

This theory has two important implications. One of these is that the same metaphor may be interpreted in different ways— as many, in fact, as there are features of connotative meaning shared by the metaphor's main constituents. We have interpreted Thomas Brown's metaphor on the grounds that blackbirds and boys share the attribute of being raucous, but other similarities could easily be adduced—liveliness, playfulness, an inclination to hide things, and so forth. It would be arbitrary, then, to insist that a metaphor has one "best" or "proper" sense; to the contrary, as many writers have noted, it is the special virtue of metaphor that it is capable of gathering unto itself several senses any one (or two, or three, or more) of which can serve as a basis for interpretation. This is a significant point because it accounts for the empirical fact that interpretations of a metaphor may exhibit wide variation even within the same speech community.

The theory before us also implies that the interpretation of a metaphor is ultimately grounded in an ability to form a concept (or two, or three, or more) which serves to establish an equivalence between the metaphor's main constituents, and of which, therefore, the constituents become exemplars par excellence. In other words, if X and Y are the constituents equated in a metaphor, interpretation requires the formation of a concept that subsumes both X and Y and thus defines the terms of their identity. Our interpretation of Brown's metaphor presupposes and derives from a concept that may be glossed as 'animate objects that are raucous.' It is essential to assume both the possibility and the validity of such a concept. Otherwise, there would be no way to account for our particular interpretation of the metaphor, or to explain the fact that it can be readily understood by others.

The concepts required to interpret a metaphor are not expressed by the metaphor itself. Rather, they may be said to underlie it and must be *discovered* through the adduction of shared features of connotative meaning. It is this act of discovery, coupled with the sometimes puzzling search that precedes it, that can make the interpretation of metaphor an original and personal experience. And it is this same act of discovery—this "finding" of a meaning that resolves the puzzle—that endows metaphor with the capacity to cause surprise, to structure the perceptions of individuals in unanticipated ways, and to make them "see" associations they have never seen before. Thus, as Herbert Read (1952:23) has written, "A metaphor is the synthesis of several units of observation into *one commanding image;* it is an expression of a complex idea, not by analysis, or by abstract statement, but by a sudden perception of an objective relation" (emphasis added).

This brings us back to where we began. The meaningful interpretation of metaphor rests upon an ability to discern some element of plausibility or truth in a statement that asserts an implausibility or falsehood. It is clear, I think, that if we can characterize this ability—or, more precisely, if we can determine how the concepts that underlie the interpretation of metaphor are formed—we will have learned something interesting about metaphor itself. We will also have learned something interesting about cultural symbols and the way they work to impose order and meaning on that elusive entity sometimes known as the "real world."

'Wise Words' as Similes

The class of Western Apache metaphors that will concern us in this essay takes the form of simple definitional utterances which represent expressions of a single surface syntactic type: subject + predicate + verb. In every case, the subject is a term designating some category of animate natural phenomena (e.g., *hada'didla':* 'lightning'; *gaagé:* 'raven'; *koyiłchoozhé:* 'carrion beetle'), the predicate is a term designating some human category (e.g., *'itsaa:* 'widow'; *'ishkiin:* 'boy'; *ndaa':* 'white man'), and the verb is a copula (*'at'éé:* 'it is', 'they are'). In every case, too, a semantic rule is violated: subject and predicate do not agree. To put it more precisely, the subject possesses designative features that are incompatible with designative features possessed by the predicate. As a result, a proposition is expressed which is contradictory and therefore always false. Eight of these metaphors are presented below:

(1) a. *hada'didla' 'ishkiin 'at'éé* ('Lightning is a boy')
   b. *gaagé 'itsaa 'at'éé* ('Ravens are widows')
   c. *koyiłchoozhé ndaa' 'at'éé* ('Carrion beetle is a white man')
   d. *góshé chaghdshé 'at'éé* ('Dogs are children')
   e. *ma' ts'ósé ndee 'at'éé* ('Apaches are coyotes')
   f. *doolé 'ichi'kíí 'at'éé* ('Butterflies are girls')
   g. *doolé 'izeegé 'at'éé* ('Butterflies are sweethearts')
   h. *túłgaiyé sáán 'at'éé* ('Burros are old women')

Metaphors of this type are identified by Western Apache as prime examples of what they call 'wise words' (*goyago yałti'*), a distinctive speech genre associated with adult men and women who have gained a reputation for balanced thinking, critical acumen, and extensive cultural knowledge. These persons, who form collectively a kind of intellectual elite, are typically well along in years and because of their advanced age are not expected to participate in the full round of daily activities that occupy most younger members of Western Apache society. Consequently, they have plenty of time for visiting and talking, especially with one another, and it is in the context of these conversational settings, called *mbaiyán daach'iłti'* ('older people talking together'), that 'wise words' are used most frequently.

When an Apache—or an ethnographer—encounters a metaphor he or she does not understand, an interpretation of it may be requested. The appropriate form of such a request is *X Y hago 'at'éégo dáłełt'ee* ('X and Y, how are they the same?'), where X stands for the subject of the metaphor and Y stands for the predicate. The appropriate response is an explanatory paraphrase that describes one or more ways in which the referents of subject and predicate are alike. I recorded sixty-four of these explanatory paraphrases—one for every metaphor listed above (1a–h) from each of eight Western Apache consultants—of which the following are representative.

(2) a. Metaphor: *hada'didla' 'ishkiin 'at'éé* ('Lightning is a boy')
   Interpretation: Yes, young boys are the same as lightning. They both dart around fast and you just can't tell

what they are going to do. They both act unpredictably. They never stay still. Both are always darting
around from place to place. They will shoot aimlessly,
too. They will both shoot anywhere, not aiming away
from people's camps, not caring what they hit. That is
why they both cause damage.

b. Metaphor: *gaagé 'itsaa 'at'éé* ('Ravens are widows')
Interpretation: Ravens are widows, these people say.
They say that because ravens and widows are poor and
don't have anyone to get meat for them. That is why
sometimes these women will stand near your camp
and wait like that until you give them food. It is the
same way with ravens. They stand around near roads
so they can eat what is killed there; they just wait like
that until some car hits something and kills it. That's
what ravens are doing when you see them standing
near roads. They are waiting to get fresh meat.

c. Metaphor: *koyiłchoozhé ndaa' 'at'éé* ('Carrion beetle
is a white man')
Interpretation: Well, there is this way that carrion
beetle reminds us of white men—they waste much
food. Carrion beetle, when he is young and before he
starts to eat meat, just eats a little hole in a leaf and
then moves on to eat a little hole in another. He
leaves plenty of good food behind him. It is like this
with some white people, too. Another way they are
the same, these two, is that in the summer they only
come out from where they live when it is cool. You
only see carrion beetles early in the morning and
again in the early evening. It is the same with some
white people. In the summer they always want to stay
some place where it is cool.

d. Metaphor: *góshé chągháshé 'at'éé* ('Dogs are children')
Interpretation: I think this way about what that
means. Both of them, children and dogs, are always
hungry. They like to eat all the time, and when they
don't get food they come to a place where someone is

cooking. There is this way, too. Both of them get into
everything and don't leave anything alone. So you
have to shoo them away. If you don't, they might
break something or soil it so you can't use it anymore.

These explanatory paraphrases, like all of the others I recorded, focus pointedly upon the specification of attributes in
terms of which the referents of the constituents in a metaphor
can be considered the same. Consequently, it seems safe to conclude that Western Apache metaphors of the type presented
here are intended to be construed *as if* they were similes, and
that failure to construe them in this manner will render interpretation extremely difficult, if not impossible. Of course, this
does not explain how the concepts underlying particular interpretations are formed, or why some interpretations are judged
more appropriate than others. I turn now to a consideration of
these problems.

Metaphorical Concepts: Designative Features

The concepts that underlie interpretations of Western Apache
metaphors consist of one feature of connotative meaning and
one or more features of designative meaning. The connotative
feature is criterial, is openly described in explanatory paraphrases, and may be viewed as the "outcome" of a search and
selection procedure (see below). The designative features are
noncriterial and are not described in explanatory paraphrases;
they are contingent upon—and therefore must be inferred
from—the position in lexical hierarchies of the semantic categories labeled by the metaphor's constituents.

Consider the following example. In paraphrase (2c) an equivalence is drawn between carrion beetles (*koyiłchoozhé*) and
white man (*ndaa'*) on the grounds that both 'waste food' (*'idáń
yo'iné'*). 'Waste food' is a feature of connotative meaning since
it does not state a necessary condition for membership in either
of the categories 'white man' or 'carrion beetle'. But 'waste food'
is only one component of the metaphorical concept. The other
components consist of two features of designative meaning that
together define a superordinate category to which both 'white

man' and 'carrion beetle' belong, namely, *ni'gosdzáń golį́į́hí*
('living things that dwell on or below the surface of the earth').
Thus the complete metaphorical concept defined by the features 'living thing' + 'earth dweller' + 'waste food', is
ni'gosdzáń golį́į́hí 'idáń yo'iné or 'living earth dwellers that
waste food'.

The designative features of a metaphorical concept are always
those features that the metaphor's constituents share by virtue
of membership in the same semantic domain. As shown by the
hierarchy depicted in figure 12, the referents of 'carrion beetle'
and 'white man' do not become members of the same domain
until the node labeled by *ni'gosdzáń golį́į́hí* ('living earth dwellers') is reached. At this point, they become exemplars of a single
category, thus overcoming and resolving the semantic con-
flict—or, in Geertz's (1964:59) phrase, the "semantic tension"—that distinguishes them at subordinate levels. It follows
that a metaphorical concept will always be *more inclusive* than
either of the categories labeled by the metaphor's constituents.
The concept 'living earth dwellers that waste food' is more inclusive than either 'carrion beetle' or 'white man'; it must be
because it subsumes them both.

The hierarchical level at which the categories labeled by a
metaphor's constituents are incorporated into the same domain
is also the lowest level at which features of connotative meaning can be adduced. This is because shared connotative features
must be compatible with designative features *shared by both
constituents,* a condition that can only be satisfied when the
referents of the constituents become exemplars of a single category. In terms of our example, this simply means that any connotative feature adduced to establish a similarity between carrion beetles and white men must be compatible with features
that define 'carrion beetle' and 'white man' as 'living earth
dwellers'. Any connotative feature that fails to meet this requirement (e.g., 'never die', 'cause snowstorms', 'make good
cooking pots') will be prohibited.

This claim is supported by empirical evidence which will be
presented later in the chapter. For the moment, however, let us
agree with R. A. Waldron (1967:174), who has observed that

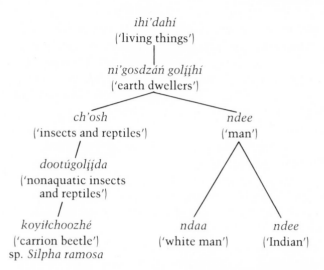

FIGURE 12. Lexical hierarchy showing location of Western Apache categories 'carrion beetle' (*koyiłchoozhé*) and 'white man' (*ndaa*).

> Metaphor is by no means carried out in total contravention of the rules [of a language] but in part by courtesy of the system itself. . . . Linguistic categorization involves classification on the basis of similarity of attributes. Metaphorical categorization is only an extension of normal linguistic activity; it is exceptionally *wide classification* [emphasis added].

The rules to which Waldron refers in this passage are what transformational grammarians commonly call "selection restrictions" (Bever and Rosenbaum 1971; Katz 1972; Katz and Fodor 1963). These rules define the conditions under which the semantic features of a language can co-occur, and therefore determine which combinations are allowable and which are not. We have hypothesized that Western Apache metaphorical concepts do not violate selection restrictions and therefore are defined by allowable combinations of semantic features.

Metaphorical Concepts: Connotative Features

The connotative features of Western Apache metaphorical concepts are chosen in compliance with a set of sociolinguistic principles which specify the *kinds of attributes* that can be adduced to establish equivalences between the referents of a metaphor's constituents. From the point of view of the individual Apache hearer, these principles constitute a heuristic strategy or plan that guides and simplifies the search for shared similarities. Simultaneously, they serve to define the criteria in terms of which the appropriateness of his or her interpretation will be assessed by other members of the speech community. The principles may be stated as follows:

A. To be appropriate, an interpretation of a Western Apache metaphor must specify one or more *behavioral attributes* which the referents of the metaphor's constituents share in common.

B. (Corollary) Interpretations that are based upon other types of attributes—such as size, shape, color, habitat, and the like—will be rejected as inappropriate.

C. To be appropriate, an interpretation of a Western Apache metaphor must specify one or more behavioral attributes that are indicative of *undesirable qualities* possessed by the referents of the metaphor's constituents.

D. (Corollary) Interpretations based upon attributes indicative of desirable qualities will be rejected as inappropriate.

The validity of principles A and C was given strong empirical support by regularities in the corpus of sixty-four explanatory paraphrases provided by my Western Apache consultants. Close examination of these statements revealed that principle A was never violated. In other words, all the paraphrases I recorded concentrated upon the identification of behavioral similarities and none adduced similarities of other kinds. Principle C was violated only twice, both times by the same consultant, and on each occasion his interpretation was challenged by older Apaches on the grounds that it "spoke too well" of the referents of the constituents of the metaphor in question.

Principles B and D were upheld by the Apaches' consistent rejection of metaphorical interpretations that violated the conditions defined by principles A and C. Discussions centering upon the reasons for such rejections were of special interest because, as shown by the three excerpts presented below, they yielded valuable information concerning the Apaches' own conceptions of how 'wise words' should be interpreted. The first excerpt, which describes an exchange between myself and two consultants, deals with the central importance of adducing behavioral similarities. So does the second, which presents a portion of a conversation between one of my consultants and his eleven-year-old daughter. The third excerpt, involving three consultants and myself, is from a discussion concerning the requirement that behavioral similarities be chosen which reflect unfavorably on the referents of a metaphor's constituents.

(3) a. CONSULTANT 1: Butterflies are girls—try that one.

   KHB: Well, this is what I think of that one—they're both the same because they're pretty, brightly colored, like the dresses the girls wear.

   CONSULTANT 2: [Laughter] You could say that, but it sounds wrong to us . . . like when you said ravens are widows because they wear black. [More laughter] Maybe they are the same that way, but to us it doesn't mean anything.

   KHB: Why not?

   CONSULTANT 1: [Long pause] It doesn't mean anything because it doesn't tell us what they *do*, these things in the 'wise words'. You have to think about how they are the same in what they do—not what they look like. Think about how they act the same. That way you'll understand it. Butterflies are girls because sometimes they act crazy, just chasing around after each other having a good time when they should be working, helping out with chores and younger children. What they look like doesn't matter, it's how they *act* that makes them the same.

   b. CONSULTANT 1 (to daughter): Who said it to you: carrion beetle is a white man?

   DAUGHTER: *X*'s wife. She said it yesterday at her camp.

   CONSULTANT 1: What did you say?

   DAUGHTER: Nothing. I didn't know what she meant.

   CONSULTANT 1: Wise words. That old woman likes to

talk that way. She wanted to know if you knew how they were the same—white men and carrion beetles. Do you know how they are the same?

DAUGHTER: No.

CONSULTANT 1: Think.

DAUGHTER: Because there are many of them.

CONSULTANT 1: [Laughter] No. Think about what they do, those two—like leaving clear tracks so they are easy to follow, or like the way they waste food.

DAUGHTER: But there *are* many of them.

CONSULTANT 1: Yes. But when old people talk like that, using 'wise words', they want you to think about how carrion beetle acts . . . then they want you to think about white men that same way. So you have to watch both of them, and then you will see how they are the same. It's what they *do* that matters. Now, do you understand?

DAUGHTER: [Pause] I think so.

c. KHB: Yesterday I was talking about 'wise words' with Y, the medicine man's wife, and she said something I didn't understand. Maybe you could help me out.

CONSULTANT 1: What did she say?

KHB: She said these old people use 'wise words' when they want to say something bad about someone.

CONSULTANT 1: What made her say that?

KHB: Well, she asked me why coyotes are Apaches and I said because they knew all about this country and were very smart.

CONSULTANT 2: [Loud laughter] Maybe what you said about coyotes is true, but it doesn't sound right to us. Coyotes are like some Apaches who don't stay home and roam around from place to place. Even at night they don't stay at home where they should be. They roam around from place to place and make lots of noise, yelling at night so you can't sleep. Some Apaches do like that too, and it's no good; they should stay at home at night and keep quiet. That way they will stay out of trouble.

CONSULTANT 3: It is true what that old woman told you. Those old people use 'wise words' when they don't like what someone has done. But they don't want to come out and use that person's name because that way he might hear about it and get angry. So they just say something like coyotes are Apaches and that is enough—everyone knows what they mean and who they are talking about.

KHB: So when you are thinking about coyotes and Apaches you look for *bad* ways that make them the same? You look for what they do that is *no good?*

CONSULTANT 2: Yes. I thought you knew that. It's the same for all 'wise words'. . . . One time when we were talking you said butterflies were girls because they were both pretty. That was wrong because it's good to look nice. I don't think butterflies are pretty, but you do, and that made us laugh. It's because they chase around after each other, like they had no work to do, that makes them the same. And that's no good.

CONSULTANT 3: Let me tell you a story. One time my mother was sick and went to the hospital in Whiteriver. It was before my older sister got married. She was supposed to look after us, cook for us. She did all right, but then one day she took off with my two [female] cousins and they went to where some people were getting ready for a dance. They stayed there all morning. Then they went to another camp to drink beer with some boys. Then they went to another camp. At night they went back to the dance. Finally, they came home. My grandmother had come to take care of us, and I guess she knew that my sister had been running around. When my sister came in my grandmother didn't say anything at first. Then she said to my older brother, "Butterflies are girls and one of them just flew in." My sister knew what it meant, I guess, because she started feeling bad. . . . That's how they use 'wise words', these old people—when they want to say something bad about someone.

It should now be apparent that the principles which govern the selection of connotative meanings are closely related to what Western Apaches conceive to be the proper use of 'wise words' in ordinary conversation. As the material presented above suggests, metaphors of this type are regarded by Apaches as vehicles for the expression of mild personal criticism. It is criticism of a highly oblique sort, however, and the identity of the person (or persons) being denounced can only be inferred from other kinds of information. This is a complex and often extremely subtle process whose analysis falls beyond the scope of the present study. What is significant here is that the requirement to select behavioral attributes—and, more specifically, behavioral attributes indicative of undesirable qualities—arises directly from the purposes 'wise words' are designed to serve and the objectives they are intended to accomplish in the course of social interaction.

Lexical Gaps and Novel Semantic Categories

Philosophers of language have long insisted that both the existence and the use of metaphor can be understood as a response to incompleteness in the vocabularies of natural languages (e.g., Alston 1964; Henle 1962; Ullman 1962; Urban 1939). No vocabulary, these scholars point out, is ever without interstices or "holes," and metaphor—because it communicates meanings that the literal senses of available words do not—functions to close or "plug" them. In this way, metaphor serves to counter what Uriel Weinreich (1964:57) has called the "designative inadequacy" of lexical systems. Simultaneously, it alleviates this deficiency through the introduction of new meanings, thus extending the semantic range of language and increasing its expressive potential.

Despite the widespread acceptance of this proposition, no systematic attempts have been made to test it (Shibles 1971). A search of the pertinent literature reveals that the validity of the proposition—or how one might go about demonstrating it—are matters which are simply not discussed. This does not seem to worry the philosophers, but for those of us who like to season our propositions with a dash or two of verification it inevitably raises doubts. In an effort to dispel such doubts, I shall present evidence here which indicates that Western Apache metaphors do, indeed, operate in the manner described above. Specifically, I will suggest that the concepts underlying these metaphors correspond to *accidental lexical gaps* in the Western Apache lexicon.

In a stimulating essay, Thomas Bever and Paul Rosenbaum (1971) have discussed the subject of lexical gaps in detail. A lexical gap is defined as any combination of semantic features that is not labeled by a lexeme. Some unlabeled combinations are prohibited by the selection restrictions of a language and in this sense may be considered *systematic* lexical gaps. Other unlabeled combinations are perfectly allowable (that is, they are not prohibited by selection restrictions) and therefore may be regarded as *accidental* lexical gaps. Our hypothesis, then, can be confirmed under two conditions. First, evidence must be presented which demonstrates that Western Apache metaphorical concepts are composed of allowable combinations of semantic features. Second, it must be shown that these concepts are not labeled by lexemes.

To test the first condition, I went through my corpus of explanatory paraphrases and made an inventory of all the concepts used by my consultants to interpret the metaphors listed in (1a–h). Then, following the procedure outlined above (pp. oo–oo), I defined these concepts in terms of their semantic components and constructed descriptions of the definitions in Western Apache ($n = 34$). Finally, I presented these descriptions to my eight Apache consultants, asking each of them if, according to his or her understanding, 'such things could be found in this world'. For example,

KHB: Living earth dwellers that waste food—from what you know, can such things be found in this world?
CONSULTANT: Yes.

An affirmative response such as this was taken to mean that the concept in question was linguistically and culturally valid—in other words, that it represented an allowable combination of semantic features and that it denoted a class of objects that existed, or could exist, within the Western Apache universe. A negative reply would have been taken to mean just the opposite. In fact, however, there were no negative replies. My consultants were unanimous in their agreement that all of the definitional phrases made clear and legitimate reference to 'things found in this world'. On the basis of this unblemished consensus, I conclude that Western Apache metaphorical concepts do not violate selection restrictions and are composed of allowable combinations of semantic features. This satisfies the first condition of our hypothesis.

To test the second condition, I began by asking my consultants if the definitional phrases could be said in shortened form. For example,

KHB: Living earth dwellers that waste food. This, what I have just said, can it be said in a short way and still mean the same?

CONSULTANT: No, I don't know of a short way to say it.

This query, which was designed to elicit synonyms or near synonyms that were also unitary lexemes, met with only two positive replies. One consultant explained that the phrase 'living earth dwellers that act fearlessly' (ni'gosdzáń gołįįhí doobiłgoyééda) could be replaced by the term doobiłgoyééhí ('fearless things'). Another consultant said that doogoyadahí ('mindless things') could be substituted for 'living earth dwellers that act mindlessly' (ni'gosdzáń gołįįhí doogoyada).

I also asked my consultants if the referents of the definitional phrases had 'names' (bízhi'). For example,

KHB: Earth dwellers that waste food—do these things have a name?

CONSULTANT: No, they have no name, just what you have called them.

In Western Apache, a name, whether it denotes a person, animal, supernatural power, or whatever, typically consists of a unitary lexeme, and for this reason my query was understood as a request to provide linguistic forms that were shorter than the rather lengthy concept labels I had composed. The query was successful in uncovering only four names, all of which were unitary lexemes.

It is obvious from these two bodies of evidence that a high

percentage of the metaphorical concepts in our sample are not lexically coded. This establishes the second condition of our hypothesis and, together with the evidence presented earlier in support of the first condition, serves to substantiate our claim that Western Apache metaphorical concepts probably correspond to accidental lexical gaps.

This finding has several important implications. One of these is that the interpretation of most Western Apache metaphors—and, I would venture to guess, the interpretation of most metaphors that take the form of disguised or hidden similes—requires of the individual an ability to form *novel semantic categories*. This must be so since the concepts that make interpretation possible are not lexically coded and therefore are not accessible through the meanings of existing vocabulary items. Almost certainly, it was this lack of accessibility that Aristotle had in mind when he said that metaphor—and here, of course, I am assuming he meant metaphorical concepts—could not be learned from others.

One can, of course, receive instruction in how to interpret metaphors from other people. This is what explanatory paraphrases and some English professors are all about. But because metaphorical concepts lack names, such coaching is inevitably circuitous. Consequently, even with instruction (and most assuredly without it) metaphorical concepts must be attained on one's own through private acts of discovery and recognition that reveal the existence of relationships where previously none were perceived. Such acts are *creative* in the fullest and most genuine sense, for they presuppose and exemplify an ability to arrange familiar semantic features into unfamiliar combinations, to form fresh categorizations of not so fresh phenomena—in short, to generate new categories of meanings.

Once again Aristotle perceived the fundamental point, this time when he observed

> Most smart sayings are derived from metaphor and thus from misleading the hearer beforehand. For it becomes evident to him that he has learned something when the conclusion turns out contrary to his expectations, and his mind seems to say, "How true it is! but up to now I missed it" (*Rhetoric* 3).

It is the rare gift of the maker of metaphor—the "mark of genius" that Aristotle so admired—that he or she glimpses new categories of meaning before anyone else and, realizing that available linguistic resources are inadequate to express them directly, turns to metaphor as a way to escape the dilemma. The task is not an easy one, however, for by voicing a proposition that is literally false he or she runs the risk of being completely misunderstood. The maker of metaphor speaks in semantic contradictions and extends to others an invitation to resolve them. If the invitation is accepted, and if attempts at resolution are successful, the result is the acquisition of a concept that is in a very real sense unspeakable. Herein lies the essential ambiguity of metaphor and also its ultimate force—it "says" with ordinary words what ordinary words alone cannot say, thus facilitating the conversion of apparent absurdity into understandable truth.

Clifford Geertz (1964 : 59) has spoken to this same point but in a slightly different way.

The power of metaphor derives precisely from the interplay between the discordant meanings it symbolically coerces into a unitary conceptual framework and from the degree to which that coercion is successful in overcoming the psychic resistance such semantic tension inevitably generates in anyone in a position to perceive it. When it works, a metaphor transforms a false identification . . . into an apt analogy; when it misfires it is a mere extravagance.

Toward a Theory of Metaphor

At the outset of this essay, I claimed that transformational linguistic theory could not explain the ability of human beings to produce and understand figurative speech. I also claimed that the transformational model excluded certain types of information that are essential to an adequate theory of metaphor. In conclusion, I would like to return to these issues and discuss them in relation to the foregoing analysis of Western Apache 'wise words'.

Let us suppose that we have in hand (or in head) a transformational grammar of the Western Apache language consisting of a syntactic component and a semantic component which conform in all respects to the specifications set down by Chomsky (1965) and Jerrold Katz (1972). Let us also suppose that we are presented with the sentence *hada'didla' 'ishkiin 'at'éé* ('Lightning is a boy') and are asked to interpret it. How would our grammar respond? What would it tell us? It would respond by assigning the sentence a literal meaning. Specifically, it would inform us that the sentence is contradictory because the subject possesses semantic features that are incompatible with features possessed by the predicate (e.g., 'sky dweller' vs. 'earth dweller'). This is *all* our grammar could accomplish. A figurative reading of the sentence would be out of the question. Why?

The inability of our grammar to provide figurative readings is directly related to a guiding principle of transformational linguistics which states that the goal of semantic theory should be to predict and explain the *properties and relations of sentence types*. "A semantic theory," according to Katz (1972:7), "must explain why the meaning of a linguistic construction makes it a case of a certain property or relation, makes it exhibit the phenomenon of synonymy, ambiguity, contradictoriness, and so forth." Such a theory, Katz (1972:62) goes on to say, "must abstract away from features of utterance contexts and concern itself with inherent features of sentence types."

This conception of the aims of semantic theory is coupled with a principle by means of which transformationalists determine what constitutes "semantic" information and what does not. Katz (1972:285–86) describes this principle as follows:

> Semantic theory offers . . . a principle telling when a piece of information is part of the meaning of a lexical item, as opposed to being a factual comment on its referent. Given such a principle, each piece of information that qualifies as semantic by the principle enters the semantic representation of that item in the form of a semantic marker in one of the lexical readings in its dictionary entry. . . . This principle, then, must decide how to choose between two lexical readings R_1 and R_2, which are the same except that R_2 contains *(ex hypothesi)* a component, putative semantic marker μ, that represents *factual* information and R_1 does not contain μ. . . . Linguistics should resist the addition

of any information to a lexical reading if its inclusion would fail to increase the predictive or explanatory power of the lexical reading and thus of the dictionary. Since what must be predicted and explained by a dictionary, as part of the semantic component of a grammar, are the semantic properties and relations of anomaly, synonymy, analyticity, entailment, etc., by showing that R_2 does not predict or explain any of these properties or relations that are not already predicted and explained by R_1, it will be shown that μ, which is the only difference between R_1 and R_2, represents factual, not semantic, information. . . . If we cannot eliminate information from the lexical reading of a word W without losing predictions and explanations of properties and relations of expressions in which W occurs, then such information belongs in the dictionary entry for W and is hence rightly deemed semantic; and if we can simplify the entries of the dictionary by excluding a certain piece of information from all of them, then it is rightly deemed nonsemantic.

In actual practice, the principle Katz discusses is used by transformational grammarians to exclude from dictionary entries all "factual comments" about the referents of lexical items. Such information is considered "nonsemantic" because it is not needed to explain the properties and relations of sentence types. For example, with respect to *hada'didla' 'ishkiin 'at'éé* ('Lightning is a boy'), the fact that both boys and lightning 'dart around' (*nánlyeed*) is not necessary to demonstrate that the sentence as a type exhibits the property of contradictoriness. In this way, transformationalists have defined as extraneous to semantic theory what we have been calling connotative meanings or, as Katz (1972:451) puts it, "the contingent properties that groups of people think belong to the referents of words." In so doing, they have committed themselves to a rigidly literalist view of language in which figurative speech has no place and cannot be explained. A theory of metaphor is ipso facto impossible. Is it any wonder that our grammar of Western Apache can tell us only that 'Lightning is a boy' embodies a semantic contradiction, or, as Uriel Weinreich (1966:399) has observed, that transformationalists have been constrained to deal with "special cases of speech—humorless, prosaic, banal prose?"

It would be a serious mistake, however, to conclude that transformational theory is irrelevant to a theory of metaphor. On the contrary, it can play a significant role. For reasons that should now be clear, a theory of metaphor must be capable of assigning to the constituents of a metaphorical expression their literal or designative meanings. To the extent that a transformational grammar specifies these meanings, it forms a necessary part of a theory of metaphor. Also, since metaphor involves the violation of certain selection restrictions, a theory of metaphor must be capable of identifying the restrictions that are violated. Transformational grammar can accomplish this task with considerable precision (at least in principle) and for this reason, too, is needed in a theory of metaphor. It is apparent, however, that a theory of metaphor must do more than specify the literal meanings of words and the rules determining their co-occurrence; it must also account for the adduction of connotative meanings and specify the rules that govern their combination with designative meanings to form metaphorical concepts. It is this last set of requirements that a transformational grammar does not satisfy.

But let us suppose it did. For the sake of argument, let us imagine that our hypothetical Western Apache grammar contains a complete listing of designative and connotative features for every item in the lexicon, as well as a full set of selection restrictions that define the conditions under which these features can be combined. Could we now assign a figurative interpretation to 'Lightning is a boy'? We might, but we would have no assurance whatsoever that our interpretation would be culturally appropriate, for nowhere in our grammar is it stated that the connotative meanings adduced to interpret a Western Apache metaphor must be commensurate with behavioral attributes that reflect unfavorably upon the referents of the metaphor's constituents. This vital information is omitted entirely, and its absence points to another weakness in the transformational paradigm: a total neglect of the cultural norms and attitudes that influence the ways in which language is *used*.

This neglect is an unfortunate consequence of the transformationalist dictum that a theory of linguistic competence should concern itself exclusively with sentence types and ignore both sentence tokens and the contexts in which they occur. Such a proscription serves to disengage the study of language from social life, and it neatly removes from consideration and analysis all forms of knowledge that guide and shape the activity of speaking, the actual conduct of verbal communication. Gone at a blow are the skills that enable the members of a speech community to decide on what should be said and how to say it, to whom it should be said and under what circumstances, and how what is said should be interpreted. Gone, in other words, are the kinds of sociolinguistic principles that complement grammatical knowledge but go beyond it to define what is proper, fitting, and as we have seen in the case of the Western Apache, fundamental to the evaluation of metaphorical speech. Gone is what Karl Teeter (1970) has called the *command* of language, the ability to call upon it and apply it in ways that meet the standards and expectations of fellow speakers. Wrenched from their natural context like so many fish out of water and hung up for sale, the sentence types prized by transformationalists are arrayed and analyzed as if they had no place of origin, no relationship to the affairs of humans, no purpose but to be dissected and, once laid open, awarded to the cleverest bidder. They exist in an ecological vacuum, isolated and unconnected, their formal properties and relations still intact, but their appropriateness—if ever they had any—a quality of no importance, a matter of no concern.

The drawbacks inherent in such an approach emerge most clearly when we consider metaphor in relation to the concept of linguistic competence. Chomsky (1965) restricts competence to the tacit knowledge represented in a grammar, that is, to the body of rules and information that enables a speaker-hearer to generate and interpret an infinite number of novel, well-formed sentences. It is in this sense, of course, that he has characterized language as a productive and creative system. Note, however, that if we accept Chomsky's definition we are obliged to conclude that because Western Apache metaphors are designatively ill-formed they constitute evidence of flawed or imperfect competence and therefore reflect *deficiencies* or *defects* in the Apaches' "knowledge" of their language. In this view, metaphors are reduced to the level of linguistic *errors* or *mistakes* not unlike those a child might make. And far from being regarded as manifestations of a creative skill, they can be taken as indicative of just the opposite: an inability to speak according to grammatical rules. Here is a real dilemma. Either we declare all Apaches who use metaphor to be linguistic incompetents, or we admit that the concept of competence as defined by Chomsky (1965) is unsatisfactory and in need of modification. The latter is clearly the only alternative.

What is needed, as Hymes (1967, 1971, 1972, 1973) has suggested, is an expansion of the concept of linguistic competence to include the ability to speak *appropriately* as well as grammatically. The two should not be confused because appropriate speech is often ungrammatical and grammatical speech is frequently inappropriate. Part of an Apache's sociolinguistic competence is to know when it is appropriate to violate grammatical rules and which rules are appropriate to violate. It is this kind of knowledge that he or she acts upon when speaking metaphorically. 'Wise words' are prime examples of *appropriately ill-formed* utterances.

In the broadened view of competence Hymes proposed, metaphor would no longer count as a linguistic blunder; neither would it imply impaired linguistic knowledge. To the contrary, it would be seen as a positive achievement, a linguistic invention won through the artful exploitation of connotative meaning and a willingness to challenge grammatical authority. Such exploitation and challenge is not for linguistic cripples; it is for persons whose competence allows them to experiment with linguistic principles in unorthodox ways. Since this ability presupposes intimate familiarity with the principles themselves, metaphor implies mastery of language rather than ineptness.

If the study of metaphor can contribute to a widened interpretation of linguistic competence, it can also contribute to a deeper appreciation of linguistic creativity. Chomsky (1965) has equated creativity with the ability of human beings to produce and understand an infinite set of novel utterances. Metaphor, on the other hand, entails the invention and acquisition of novel semantic categories. The two abilities, though related, are not the same. The former, as Hymes (1973 : 119) has pointed out, is basically concerned with the "systemic potentiality" of language, while the latter is "that kind of creativity which consists of the discovery of possibilities implicit in a [linguistic] system, but not yet discovered, not yet known" (Hymes 1973 : 99). Creativity in Chomsky's sense consists in the unfolding of existing structures. Creativity in metaphor consists in the use of existing structures to forge new ones.

What distinguishes the two even more sharply, I think, is that the former is achieved through adherence to grammatical rules while the latter is achieved by breaking them. Chomsky's type of creativity manifests itself in the form of utterances which, novel though they may be, do not depart from established canons of designative meaning. In contrast, metaphor flaunts these canons in order to capitalize on connotative meanings and expresses what designative meanings cannot. Herein lies a fundamental difference. The transformationalist's ideal speaker-hearer is consistently obedient to the strictly grammatical rules of language. The maker of metaphor is not.

As defined by Chomsky, creativity is commensurate with one form of "unboundedness" in language, that is, with the ability of individuals to make continuously original use of materials already present. Metaphor entails this ability, too, but *adds* to what is present by formulating and sponsoring new categories of meaning. In so doing, it functions to augment the lexical semantic resources of linguistic systems and serves as an indispensable device for adapting these systems to the changing communicative needs of their speakers.

It hardly needs to be said that anthropologists owe a great intellectual debt to Noam Chomsky and his insight into parts of a theory of language. But metaphor cannot be ignored, and Chomsky's theory, though necessary to an explanation of it, is not sufficient. What the Western Apache tells us is true. Ravens *are* widows and lightning *is* a boy. *I* am a carrion beetle. And it is important to find out why. Our best hope for success lies in continuing to do ethnography, and this means trying to make sense of contingent facts, unlabeled semantic categories, rules for language use, and the like. For it is in metaphor—perhaps more dramatically than in any other form of symbolic expression—that language and culture come together and display their fundamental inseparability. A theory of one that excludes the other will inevitably do damage to both.

In closing, it is well to keep in mind that well-turned metaphors are recognized and appreciated by persons other than ethnographers, philosophers of language, and literary critics. Shortly before I last departed from the field, one of my Western Apache consultants, who was standing by as I packed my belongings, suggested that I stop for a moment—there was something he wanted to tell me:

> It's too bad that you didn't try to learn about 'wise words' before. When I was young, old people around here used to make them up all the time. Only a few of them did it and they were the best talkers of all. Some people would try but they couldn't do it so they stopped trying. Now you know what some 'wise words' mean—that's what you asked us to teach you. But you still haven't made any up. Maybe those old people would have taught you how they did it. It's hard to do and you have to know a lot about everything. Those old people were smart. One of them would make up a new one and right away other people would start to use it. They had never heard it before and if it was a good one it would make them happy and they would laugh. It's still that way when someone makes one up. Only the good talkers can make them up like that. They are the ones who *really* speak Apache. They are the ones who make up 'wise words' and don't have to use someone else's. I don't know how they do it. It's something special that they know.

5 / 'To Give Up on Words': Silence in Western Apache Culture

It is not the case that a man who is silent says nothing.
ANONYMOUS

Anyone who has read about American Indians has probably encountered statements which impute to them a strong predilection for keeping silent or, as one writer has put it, "a fierce reluctance to speak except when absolute necessary." In the popular literature, where this characterization is particularly widespread, it is commonly portrayed as the outgrowth of such dubious causes as "instinctive dignity," "an impoverished language," or perhaps worst of all, the Indians' "lack of personal warmth." Although statements of this sort are plainly erroneous and dangerously misleading, it is noteworthy that professional anthropologists have made few attempts to correct them. Traditionally, ethnographers and linguists have paid little attention to cultural interpretations given to silence or, equally important, to the types of social contexts in which it regularly occurs.

This study investigates certain aspects of silence in Western Apache culture. After considering some of the theoretical issues involved, I will briefly describe a number of situations—recurrent in Western Apache society—in which one or more of the participants typically refrain from speech for lengthy periods of time.[1] This is accompanied by a discussion of how such acts of silence are interpreted and why they are encouraged and deemed appropriate. I conclude by advancing a hypothesis that accounts for the reasons that the Western Apache refrain from speaking when they do, and I suggest that, with proper testing, this hypothesis may be shown to have relevance to silence behavior in other cultures.

Silence and Speech

A basic finding of sociolinguistics is that, although both language and language usage are structured, it is the latter which responds most sensitively to extralinguistic influences. Accordingly, a number of studies have addressed themselves to the problem of how factors in the social environment of speech events delimit the range and condition the selection of message forms (cf. Brown and Gilman 1960; Ervin-Tripp 1967; Frake 1964; Friedrich 1966; Gumperz 1961). These studies may be viewed as taking the position that verbal communication is fundamentally a decision-making process in which a speaker, having elected to speak, selects from among a repertoire of available codes that which is most appropriately suited to the situation at hand. Once a code has been selected, the speaker picks a suitable channel of transmission and then, finally, makes a choice from a set of referentially equivalent expressions within the code. The intelligibility of the expression he or she chooses will, of course, be subject to grammatical constraints. But its acceptability will not. Rules for the selection of linguistic alternates operate on features of the social environment and are commensurate with rules governing the conduct of face-to-face interaction. As such, they are properly conceptualized as lying outside the structure of language itself.

It follows from this that for a stranger to communicate appropriately with the members of an unfamiliar society it is not enough that he or she learn to formulate messages intelligibly. Something else is needed: a knowledge of what kinds of codes, channels, and expressions to use in what kinds of situations and to what kinds of people—as Dell Hymes (1962, 1964) has termed it, an "ethnography of communication."

There is considerable evidence to suggest that extra-linguistic factors influence not only the use of speech but its actual occurrence as well. In our own culture, for example, remarks such as "Don't you know when to keep quiet?" "Don't talk until you're introduced," and "Remember now, no talking in church" all point to the fact that an individual's decision to speak may be directly contingent upon the character of his or her surroundings. Few of us would maintain that "silence is golden" for all people at all times. But we feel that silence is a virtue for some people some of the time, and we encourage children on the road to cultural competence to act accordingly.

Although the form of silence is always the same, the function of a specific act of silence—that is, its interpretation by and effect upon other people—will vary according to the social context in which it occurs. For example, if I choose to keep silent in the chambers of a justice of the Supreme Court, my action is likely to be interpreted as a sign of politeness or respect. On the other hand, if I refrain from speaking to an established friend or colleague, I am apt to be accused of rudeness or harboring a grudge. In one instance, my behavior is judged by others to be correct or fitting; in the other, it is criticized as being out of line.

The point, I think, is fairly obvious. For a stranger entering an alien society, a knowledge of when *not* to speak may be as basic to the production of culturally acceptable behavior as a knowledge of what to say. It stands to reason, then, that an adequate ethnography of communication should not confine itself exclusively to the analysis of choice within verbal repertoires. It should also specify those conditions under which the members of the society regularly decide to refrain from verbal behavior altogether.

Silence in Social Context

The research on which this paper is based was conducted over a period of sixteen months (1964–69) in the Western Apache settlement of Cibecue. Cibecue's 850 residents participate in an unstable economy that combines subsistence agriculture, cattle raising, sporadic wage earning, and government subsidies in the form of welfare checks and social security benefits. Unemployment is a serious problem, and substandard living conditions are widespread.

Although reservation life has precipitated far-reaching changes in the composition and geographical distribution of Western Apache social groups, consanguineal kinship—real and imputed—remains the single most powerful force in the establishment and regulation of interpersonal relationships. The focus of domestic activity is the individual 'camp' *gowǫ*. This term labels both the occupants and the location of a single dwelling or, as is more apt to be the case, several dwellings built within a few feet of each other. The majority of *gowǫ* in Cibecue are occupied by nuclear families. The next largest residential unit is the *gotáh* ('camp cluster'), which is a group of spatially localized *gowǫ*, each having at least one adult member who is related by ties of matrilineal kinship to persons living in all the others. An intricate system of exogamous clans serves to extend kinship relationships beyond the *gowǫ* and *gotáh* and facilitates concerted action in projects, most notably the presentation of ceremonials, requiring large amounts of manpower. Despite the presence in Cibecue of a variety of Anglo missionaries and a dwindling number of medicine men, diagnostic and curing rituals, as well as the girls' puberty ceremonial, continue to be performed with regularity. Witchcraft persists in undiluted form.

Of the many broad categories of events, or scenes, that comprise the daily round of Western Apache life, I shall deal here only with those that are coterminous with what Erving Goffman (1961, 1963) has termed "focused gatherings" or "encounters." The concept *situation*, in keeping with established usage, will refer inclusively to the location of such a gathering, its physical setting, its point in time, the standing behavior patterns that accompany it, and the social attributes of the persons involved (Ervin-Tripp 1967; Hymes 1962, 1964).

In what follows, however, I will be mainly concerned with the roles and statuses of participants. The reason for this is that the critical factor in the Apache's decision to speak or keep silent seems always to be the nature of his or her relationships to other people. To be sure, other features of the situation are significant, but apparently only to the extent that they influence the perception of status and role. What this implies, of course, is that roles and statuses are not fixed attributes. Although they may be depicted as such in a static model (and often with good reason), they are appraised and acted upon in particular social contexts and, as a result, are subject to redefinition and variation.[2] With this in mind, let us now turn our attention to the Western Apache and the types of situations in which, as one of my consultants put it, "it is right to give up on words."

1. 'Meeting strangers' (*'adahyé nagahahí bidedeyaa*). The term *'adahyé nagahahí* labels categories at two levels of contrast. At the most general level, it designates any person—Apache or non-Apache—who, prior to an initial meeting, has never been seen and therefore cannot be identified. In addition, the term is used to refer to Apaches who, though previously seen and known by some external criteria such as clan affiliation or personal name, have never been engaged in face-to-face interaction. The latter category, which is more restricted than the first, typically includes individuals who live on the adjacent San Carlos reservation, in Fort Apache settlements geographically removed from Cibecue, and those who fall into the category *doohwak'iida* (non-kinsmen). In all cases, strangers are separated by social distance. And in all cases it is considered appropriate, when encountering them for the first time, to refrain from speaking.

The type of situation described as 'meeting strangers' (*'adahyé nagahahí bidedeyaa*) can take place in any number of different physical settings. However, it occurs most frequently in the context of events such as fairs and rodeos, which, owing to the large number of people in attendance, offer unusual opportunities for chance encounters. In large gatherings, the lack of verbal communication between strangers is apt to go unnoticed, but in smaller groups it becomes quite conspicuous. The following incident, involving two strangers who found themselves part of a four-man roundup crew, serves as a good example. My consultant, who was also a member of the crew, recalled the following episode:

> One time, I was with A, B, and x down at Gleason Flat, working cattle. That man, x, was from East Fork [a community nearly forty miles from Cibecue] where B's wife was from. But he didn't know A, never knew him before, I guess. First day, I worked with x. At night, when we camped, we talked with B, but x and A didn't say anything to each other. Same way, second day. Same way, third. Then, at night on fourth day, we were sit-

ting by the fire. Still, x and A didn't talk. Then A said, "Well, I
know there is a stranger to me here, but I've been watching him
and I know he is all right." After that, x and A talked a lot. . . .
Those two men didn't know each other, so they took it easy
at first.

As this incident suggests, the Western Apache do not feel
compelled to "introduce" persons who are unknown to each
other. Eventually, it is assumed, strangers will begin to speak.
However, this is a decision that is properly left to the individuals involved, and no attempt is made to hasten it. Outside help
in the form of introductions or other verbal routines is viewed
as presumptuous and unnecessary.

Strangers who are quick to launch into conversation are frequently eyed with undisguised suspicion. A typical reaction
to such individuals is that they "want something," that is,
their willingness to violate convention is attributed to some
urgent need which is likely to result in requests for money, la-
bor, or transportation. Another common reaction to talkative
strangers is that they are intoxicated.

If the stranger is an Anglo, it is usually assumed that he
"wants to teach us something" (i.e., give orders or instructions)
or that he "wants to make friends in a hurry." The latter response is especially revealing, since Western Apaches are extremely reluctant to be hurried into friendships—with Anglos
or each other. Their verbal reticence with strangers is directly
related to the conviction that the establishment of social relationships is a serious matter that calls for caution, careful judgment, and plenty of time.

2. 'Courting' (ⁿiigoláá). During the initial stages of courtship,
young men and women go without speaking for conspicuous
lengths of time. Courting may occur in a wide variety of settings—practically anywhere, in fact—and at virtually any time
of the day or night, but it is most readily observable at large
public gatherings such as ceremonials, wakes, and rodeos. At
these events, 'sweethearts' ('izeegé) may stand or sit (sometimes holding hands) for as long as an hour without exchanging a word. I have been told by adult consultants that the

young people's reluctance to speak may become even more pronounced in situations where they find themselves alone.

Apaches who have just begun to court attribute their silence
to 'intense shyness' (*histe'*) and a feeling of acute 'self-con-
sciousness' (*dayéézi*) which, they claim, stems from their lack
of familiarity with one another. More specifically, they complain of "not knowing what to do" in each other's presence and
of the fear that whatever they say, no matter how well thought
out in advance, will sound "dumb" or "stupid."

One consultant, a youth seventeen years old, commented as
follows:

> It's hard to talk with your sweetheart at first. She doesn't
> know you and won't know what to say. It's the same way to-
> wards her. You don't know how to talk yet . . . so you get very
> bashful. That makes it sometimes so you don't say anything. So
> you just go around together and don't talk. At first, it's better
> that way. Then, after a while, when you know each other, you
> aren't shy anymore and can talk good.

The Western Apache draw an equation between the ease and
frequency with which a young couple talks and how well they
know each other. Thus, it is expected that after several months
of steady companionship sweethearts will start to have lengthy
conversations. Earlier in their relationship, however, protracted
discussions may be openly discouraged. This is especially true
for girls, who are informed by their mothers and older sisters
that silence in courtship is a sign of modesty and that an eager-
ness to speak betrays previous experience with men. In extreme
cases, they add, it may be interpreted as a willingness to engage
in sexual relations. Said one woman, aged thirty-two:

> This way I have talked to my daughter. "Take it easy when
> boys come around this camp and want you to go somewhere
> with them. When they talk to you, just listen at first. Maybe
> you won't know what to say. So don't talk about just anything.
> If you talk with these boys right away, then they will know you
> know all about them. They will think you've been with many
> boys before, and they will start talking about that."

3. 'Children coming home' (chạgháshé naakai). The Western Apache lexeme 'iłta'naadzaa ('reunion') is used to describe encounters between an individual who has returned home after a long absence and his relatives and friends. The most common type of reunion, chạgháshé naakai ('children coming home'), involves boarding school students and their parents. It occurs in late May or early in June, and its setting is usually a trading post or school, where parents congregate to await the arrival of buses bringing the children home. As the latter disembark and locate their parents in the crowd, one anticipates a flurry of verbal greetings. Typically, however, there are few or none at all. Indeed, it is not unusual for parents and child to go without speaking for as long as fifteen minutes.

When the silence is broken, it is almost always the child who breaks it. Parents listen attentively to everything he or she says but speak hardly at all themselves. This pattern persists even after the family has reached the privacy of its camp, and two or three days may pass before the child's parents seek to engage him or her in sustained conversation.

According to my consultants, the silence of Western Apache parents at (and after) reunions with their children is ultimately predicated on the possibility that the latter have been adversely affected by their experiences away from home. Uppermost is the fear that, as a result of protracted exposure to Anglo attitudes and values, the children have come to view their parents as ignorant, old-fashioned, and no longer deserving of respect. One of my most thoughtful and articulate consultants commented on the problem as follows:

> You just can't tell about those children after they've been with White men for a long time. They get their minds turned around sometimes. . . . They forget where they come from and get ashamed when they come home because their parents and relatives are poor. They forget how to act with these Apaches and get mad easy. They walk around all night and get into fights. They don't stay at home.
>
> At school, some of them learn to want to be White men, so they come back and try to act that way. But we are still

Apaches! So we don't know them anymore, and it is like we never knew them. It is hard to talk to them when they are like that.

Apache parents openly admit that, initially, children who have been away to school seem distant and unfamiliar. They have grown older, of course, and their physical appearance may have changed. But more fundamental is the concern that they have acquired new ideas and expectations which will alter their behavior in unpredictable ways. No matter how pressing this concern may be, however, it is considered inappropriate to directly interrogate a child after his or her arrival home. Instead, parents anticipate that within a short time the child will begin to divulge information that will enable them to determine in what ways, if any, his or her views and attitudes have changed. This, the Apache say, is why children do practically all the talking in the hours following a reunion, and why their parents remain unusually silent.

Said one man, the father of two children who had recently returned from boarding school in Utah:

> Yes, it's right that we didn't talk much to them when they came back, my wife and me. They were away for a long time, and we didn't know how they would like it, being home. So we waited. Right away, they started to tell stories about what they did. Pretty soon we could tell they liked it, being back. That made us feel good. So it was easy to talk to them again. It was like they were before they went away.

4. 'Getting cussed out' (*shiłdit'éé*). This expression is used to describe any situation in which one individual, angered and enraged, shouts insults and criticisms at another. Although the object of such invective is in most cases the person or persons who provoked it, this is not always the case, because an Apache who is truly beside himself with rage is likely to vent his feelings on anyone whom he sees or who happens to be within range of his voice. Consequently, 'getting cussed out' may involve large numbers of people who are totally innocent of the charges being hurled against them. But whether they are inno-

cent, their response to the situation is the same. They refrain from speech.

Like the types of situations we have discussed thus far, 'getting cussed out' can occur in a wide variety of physical settings: at ceremonial dance grounds and trading posts, inside and outside wickiups and houses, on food-gathering expeditions and shopping trips—in short, wherever and whenever individuals lose control of their tempers and lash out verbally at persons nearby.

Although 'getting cussed out' is basically free of setting-imposed restrictions, the Western Apache fear it most at gatherings where alcohol is consumed. My consultants observed that especially at 'drinking parties' (naa'idląą'), where there is much rough joking and ostensibly mock criticism, it is easy for well-intentioned remarks to be misconstrued as insults. Provoked in this way, persons who are intoxicated may become hostile and launch into explosive tirades, often with no warning at all.

The silence of Apaches who are 'getting cussed out' is consistently explained in terms of the belief that individuals who are 'enraged' (hashkee) are also irrational or 'crazy' (bíní'édįh). In this condition, it is said, they "forget who they are" and become oblivious to what they say and do. Concomitantly, they lose all concern for the consequences of their actions on other people. In a word, they are dangerous. Said one consultant,

> When people get mad they get crazy. Then they start yelling and saying bad things. Some say they are going to kill somebody for what he has done. Some keep it up that way for a long time, maybe walk from camp to camp, real angry, yelling, crazy like that. They keep it up for a long time, some do.
>
> People like that don't know what they are saying, so you can't tell about them. When you see someone like that, just walk away. If he yells at you, let him say whatever he wants to. Let him say anything. Maybe he doesn't mean it. But he doesn't know that. He will be crazy, and he could try to kill you.

Another Apache said, "When someone gets mad at you and starts yelling, then just don't do anything to make him get worse. Don't try to quiet him down because he won't know why you're doing it. If you try to do that, he may just get worse and try to hurt you."

As the latter of these statements implies, the Western Apache operate on the assumption that enraged persons—because they are temporarily "crazy"—are difficult to reason with. Indeed, there is a widely held belief that attempts at mollification will serve to intensify anger, thus increasing the chances of physical violence. The appropriate strategy when 'getting cussed out' is to do nothing, to avoid any action that will attract attention to oneself. Since speaking accomplishes just the opposite, silence is strongly advised.

5. 'Being with people who are sad' (ndee bił doobiłgozhǫǫda). Although the Western Apache phrase that labels this situation has no precise equivalent in English, it refers quite specifically to gatherings in which individuals find themselves in the company of someone whose spouse or kinsman has recently died. Distinct from wakes and burials, which follow immediately after a death, 'being with people who are sad' is most likely to occur several weeks later. At this time, close relatives of the deceased emerge from a period of intense mourning (during which they rarely venture beyond the limits of their camps) and start to resume their normal activities within the community. To persons anxious to convey their sympathies, this is interpreted as a sign that visitors will be welcomed and, if possible, provided with food and drink. To those less solicitous, it means that unplanned encounters with the bereaved must be anticipated and prepared for.

'Being with people who are sad' can occur on a footpath, in a camp, at church, or in a trading post; but whatever the setting—and regardless of whether it is the result of a planned visit or an accidental meeting—the situation is marked by a minimum of speech. Queried about this, my consultants volunteered three types of explanations. The first is that persons 'who are sad' are so burdened with 'intense grief' ('ádił ńtsikęęs) that speaking requires of them an unusual amount of physical effort. It is courteous and considerate, therefore, not to attempt to engage them in conversation.

A second explanation is that in situations of this sort verbal communication is basically unnecessary. Everyone is familiar with what has happened, and talking about it, even for the purpose of conveying solace and sympathy, would only reinforce and augment the sadness felt by those who were close to the deceased. Again, for reasons of courtesy, this is something to be avoided.

The third explanation is rooted in the belief that 'intense grief', like intense rage, produces changes in the personality of the individual who experiences it. As evidence for this, numerous instances are cited in which the emotional strain of dealing with death, coupled with an overwhelming sense of irrevocable personal loss, has caused persons who were formerly mild and even-tempered to become abusive, hostile, and physically violent.

That old woman, X, who lives across Cibecue Creek, one time her first husband died. After that she cried all the time, for a long time. Then, I guess she got mean because everyone said she drank a lot and got into fights. Even with her close relatives, she did like that for a long time. She was too sad for her husband. That's what made her like that; it made her lose her mind.

My father was like that when his wife died. He just stayed home all the time and wouldn't go anywhere. He didn't talk to any of his relatives or children. He just said, "I'm hungry. Cook for me." That's all. He stayed that way for a long time. His mind was not with us. He was still with his wife.

My uncle died in 1941. His wife sure went crazy right away after that. Two days after they buried the body, we went over there and stayed with those people who had been left alone. My aunt got mad at us. She said, "Why do you come over here? You can't bring my husband back. I can take care of myself and those others in my camp, so why don't you go home." She sure was mad that time, too sad for someone who died. She didn't know what she was saying because in about one week she came to our camp and said, "My relatives, I'm all right now. When you came to help me, I had too much sadness and my mind was no good. I said bad words to you. But now I am all right and I know what I am doing."

As these statements indicate, the Western Apache assume that a person suffering from 'intense grief' is likely to be disturbed and unstable. Even though outwardly composed, they say, there is always the possibility that he or she is emotionally upset and therefore unusually prone to volatile outbursts. Apaches acknowledge that such an individual might welcome conversation in the context of 'being with people who are sad', but on the other hand they fear it might prove incendiary. Under these conditions, which resemble those of situation 4, it is considered both expedient and appropriate to keep silent.

6. 'Being with someone for whom they sing' (ndee bił bidaadistááhá). The last type of situation to be described is restricted to a small number of physical locations and is more directly influenced by temporal factors than any of the situations we have discussed so far. 'Being with someone for whom they sing' takes place only in the context of 'curing ceremonials' (goch'itał; 'édotał). These events begin early at night and come to a close shortly before dawn the following day. In the late fall and throughout the winter, curing ceremonials are held inside the patient's wickiup or house. In the spring and summer, they are located outside, at some open place near the patient's camp or at specially designated dance grounds where group rituals of all kinds are regularly performed.

Prior to the start of a curing ceremonial, all persons in attendance may feel free to talk with the patient. Conversation breaks off, however, when the patient is informed that the ceremonial is about to begin, and it ceases entirely when the presiding medicine man commences to chant. From this point on, until the completion of the final chant next morning, it is inappropriate for anyone except the medicine man (and, if he has them, his aides) to speak to the patient.

In order to appreciate the explanation Apaches give for this prescription, we must briefly discuss the concept of 'supernatural power' (diyi') and describe some of the effects it is believed to have on persons at whom it is directed. Elsewhere (Basso 1969:30) I have defined "power" as follows:

> The term (diyi') refers to one or all of a set of abstract and
> invisible forces which are said to derive from certain classes
> of animals, plants, minerals, meteorological phenomena, and
> mythological figures within the Western Apache universe. Any
> of the various powers may be acquired by man and, if properly
> handled, used for a variety of purposes.

A power that has been antagonized by disrespectful behavior towards its source may retaliate by causing the offender to become sick. 'Power-caused illnesses' (kaa sitįį diyi' bił) are properly treated with curing ceremonials in which one or more medicine men, using chants and various items of ritual paraphernalia, attempt to neutralize the sickness-causing power with powers of their own.

Roughly two thirds of my consultants asserted that a medicine man's power actually enters the body of the patient; others maintain that it merely closes in and envelops him or her. In any case, all agreed that the patient is brought into intimate contact with a potent supernatural force which produces a condition labeled godiyįh ('holy').

The term godiyįh may also be translated as 'potentially harmful' and, in this sense, is regularly used to describe classes of objects (including all sources of power) that are surrounded with taboos. In keeping with the semantics of godiyįh, the Western Apache explain that, besides making patients holy, power makes them potentially harmful. And it is this transformation, they explain, that is basically responsible for the cessation of verbal communication during curing ceremonials.

Said one consultant,

> When they start singing for someone like that, he sort of
> goes away with what the medicine man is working with [i.e.,
> power]. Sometimes people they sing for don't know you, even
> after it [the curing ceremonial] is over. They get holy, and you
> shouldn't try to talk to them when they are like that . . . it's
> best to leave them alone.

Another consultant made similar comments:

> When they sing for someone, what happens is like this: that man they sing for doesn't know why he is sick or which way to go. So the medicine man has to show him and work on him. That is when he gets holy, and that makes him go off somewhere in his mind, so you should stay away from him.

Because Apaches undergoing ceremonial treatment are perceived as having been changed by power into something different from their normal selves, they are regarded with caution and apprehension. Their newly acquired status places them in close proximity to the supernatural and, as such, carries with it a very real element of danger and uncertainty. These conditions combine to make 'being with someone for whom they sing' a situation in which speech is considered disrespectful and, if not exactly harmful, at least potentially hazardous.

Status Ambiguity and Role Expectations

Although the types of situations described above differ from one another in numerous ways, I will argue in what follows that the underlying determinants of silence are in each case basically the same. Specifically, I will advance the hypothesis that keeping silent in Western Apache culture is associated with social situations in which participants perceive their relationships with one another to be ambiguous and/or unpredictable.

Let us begin with the observation that, in all the situations we have described, *silence is defined as appropriate with respect to a specific individual or individuals*. In other words, the use of speech is not directly curtailed by the setting of a situation nor by the physical activities that accompany it but, rather, by the perceived social and psychological attributes of at least one focal participant.

It may also be observed that, in each type of situation, *the status of the focal participant is marked by ambiguity*—either because he or she is unfamiliar to other participants in the situation or because, owing to some recent event, a status formerly held has been changed or is in a process of transition.

Thus, in situation 1, persons who earlier considered themselves "strangers" move towards some other relationship, perhaps 'friend' (shit'eké), perhaps 'enemy' (shik'endiihí). In situation 2, young people who have had relatively limited exposure to one another attempt to adjust to the new and intimate status of 'sweetheart'. These two situations are similar in that the focal participants have little or no prior knowledge of each other. Their social identities are not as yet clearly defined, and their expectations, lacking the foundation of previous experience, are poorly developed.

Situation 3 is somewhat different. Although the participants—parents and their children—are well known to each other, their relationship has been seriously interrupted by the latter's prolonged absence from home. This, combined with the possibility that recent experiences at school have altered the children's attitudes, introduces a definite element of unfamiliarity and doubt. Situation 3 is not characterized by an absence of role expectations but by the participants' perception that those already in existence may be outmoded and in need of revision.

Status ambiguity is present in situation 4 because a focal participant is enraged and, as a result, considered 'crazy'. Until this individual returns to a more rational condition, others in the situation have no way of predicting how he or she will behave. Situation 5 is similar in that the personality of the focal participants is seen to have undergone a marked shift which makes their actions more difficult to anticipate. In both situations, the status of focal participants is uncertain because of real or imagined changes in their psychological makeup.

In situation 6, a focal participant is ritually transformed from an essentially neutral state to one that is contextually defined as 'potentially harmful'. Ambiguity and apprehension accompany this transition, and, as in situations 4 and 5, established patterns of interaction must be waived until the focal participant reverts to a less threatening condition.

This discussion points up a third feature characteristic of all situations: *the ambiguous status of focal participants is accompanied by either the absence or the suspension of established role expectations.* In every instance, nonfocal participants (i.e., those who refrain from speech) are uncertain of how the focal participant will behave towards them and, conversely, how they should behave towards him or her. Stated in the simplest way possible, their roles become blurred with the result that established expectations—if they exist—lose their relevance as guidelines for social action and must be temporarily discarded or abruptly modified.

We are now in a position to expand upon our initial hypothesis and make it more explicit.

1. In Western Apache culture, the absence of verbal communication is associated with social situations in which the status of focal participants is ambiguous.

2. Under these conditions, fixed role expectations lose their applicability and the illusion of predictability in social interaction is lost.

3. To sum up and reiterate: keeping silent among the Western Apache is a response to uncertainty and unpredictability in social relations.

Cross-Cultural Regularities

The question remains to what extent the foregoing hypothesis helps to account for silence behavior in other cultures. Unfortunately, it is impossible at the present time to provide anything approaching a conclusive answer. Standard ethnographies contain very little information about the circumstances under which verbal communication is discouraged, and it is only within the past few years that problems of this sort have engaged the attention of sociolinguists. The result is that adequate cross-cultural data are almost completely lacking.

As a first step towards the elimination of this deficiency, an attempt was made to investigate the occurrence and interpretation of silence in other Indian societies of the American Southwest. Our findings at this early stage, though neither fully representative nor sufficiently comprehensive, are extremely suggestive. By way of illustration, I quote below from portions of a preliminary report prepared by Priscilla Mowrer (1970), herself a Navajo, who inquired into the situational features of Navajo silence behavior in the vicinity of Tuba City on the Navajo reservation in east-central Arizona.

I. SILENCE AND COURTING: Navajo youngsters of opposite sexes just getting to know one another say nothing, except to sit close together and maybe hold hands. . . . In public, they may try not to let on that they are interested in each other, but in private it is another matter. If the girl is at a gathering where the boy is also present, she may go off by herself. Falling in step, the boy will generally follow. They may just walk around or find some place to sit down. But, at first, they will not say anything to each other.

II. SILENCE AND LONG ABSENT RELATIVES: When a male or female relative returns home after being gone for six months or more, he (or she) is first greeted with a handshake. If the returnee is male, the female greeter may embrace him and cry—the male, meanwhile, will remain dry-eyed and silent.

III. SILENCE AND ANGER: The Navajo tend to remain silent when being shouted at by a drunk or angered individual because that particular individual is considered temporarily insane. To speak to such an individual, the Navajo believe, just tends to make the situation worse. . . . People remain silent because they believe that the individual is not himself, that he may have been witched, and is not responsible for the change in his behavior.

IV. SILENT MOURNING: Navajos speak very little when mourning the death of a relative. . . . The Navajo mourn and cry together in pairs. Men will embrace one another and cry together. Women, however, will hold one another's hands and cry together.

V. SILENCE AND THE CEREMONIAL PATIENT: The Navajo consider it wrong to talk to a person being sung over. The only people who talk to the patient are the medicine man and a female relative (or male relative if the patient is male) who is in charge of food preparation. The only time the patient speaks openly is when the medicine man asks her (or him) to pray along with him.

These observations suggest that striking similarities may exist between the types of social contexts in which Navajos and Western Apaches refrain from speech. If this impression is confirmed by further research, it will lend obvious cross-cultural support to the hypothesis advanced above. But regardless of the final outcome, the situational determinants of silence seem eminently deserving of further study. For as we become better informed about the types of contextual variables that mitigate against the use of verbal codes, we should also learn more about those variables that encourage and promote them.

6 / 'Stalking with Stories': Names, Places, and Moral Narratives Among the Western Apache

Shortly before his death in 1960, Clyde Kluckhohn made the following observation in a course he gave at Harvard University on the history of anthropological thought: "The most interesting claims people make are those they make about themselves. Cultural anthropologists should keep this in mind, especially when they are doing fieldwork." Although Kluckhohn's comment seemed tenuously connected to the topic of his lecture (he was speaking that day on the use of statistical methods in culture and personality studies), few of his students were distracted or annoyed. We had discovered early on that some of his most provocative thoughts were likely to come in the form of brief asides delivered casually and without apology at unexpected moments. We also learned that these ostensibly offhand remarks frequently contained advice on a topic that we were eager to know more about: ethnography and ethnographic research. Rarely, however, did Kluckhohn see fit to elaborate on his advice, and so it was only later, after some of us had become ethnographers ourselves, that we could begin to assess it properly.

I think that in this particular instance Kluckhohn was right. Attending carefully to claims that people make about themselves, and then trying to grasp with some exactness what they have claimed and why, can be a perplexing and time-consuming business. But when the work goes well—when puzzling claims are seen to make principled sense and when, as a consequence of this, one is able to move closer to an understanding of who the people involved imagine themselves to be—it can be richly informative and highly worthwhile. Indeed, as Kluckhohn implied in his textbook *Mirror for Man* (1949), it is just this sort of work that makes ethnography the singularly valuable activity—and, he might have added, the singularly arresting and gratifying one—it very often is.

This essay focuses on a small set of spoken texts in which members of a contemporary American Indian society express claims about themselves, their language, and the lands on which they live. Specifically, I shall be concerned here with a set of statements made by men and women from Cibecue. The statements that interest me, which could be supplemented by a large number of others, are the following.

1. The land is always stalking people. The land makes people live right. The land looks after us. The land looks after people [Mrs. Annie Peaches, age 77, 1977].

2. Our children are losing the land. It doesn't go to work on them anymore. They don't know the stories about what happened at these places. That's why some get into trouble [Mr. Ronnie Lupe, age 42, chairman, White Mountain Apache Tribe, 1978].

3. We used to survive only off the land. Now it's no longer that way. Now we live only with money, so we need jobs. But the land still looks after us. We know the names of the places where everything happened. So we stay away from badness [Mr. Nick Thompson, age 64, 1980].

4. I think of that mountain called 'white rocks lie above in a compact cluster' as if it were my maternal grandmother. I recall stories of how it once was at that mountain. The stories told to me were like arrows. Elsewhere, hearing that mountain's name, I see it. Its name is like a picture. Stories go to work on you like arrows. Stories make you live right. Stories make you replace yourself [Mr. Benson Lewis, age 64, 1979].

5. One time I went to L.A., training for mechanic. It was no good, sure no good. I start drinking, hang around bars all the time. I start getting into trouble with my wife, fight sometimes with her. It was *bad*. I forget about this country here around Cibecue. I forget all the names and stories. I don't hear them in

my mind anymore. I forget how to live right, forget how to be
strong [Mr. Wilson Lavender, age 52, 1975].

If the texts of these statements resist quick and easy interpretation, it is not because the people who made them are confused or cloudy thinkers. Neither is it because, as one unfortunate commentator would have us believe, the Western Apache
are "mystically inclined and correspondingly inarticulate." The
problem we face is a semiotic one, a barrier to constructing appropriate sense and significance. It arises from the obvious circumstance that all views articulated by Apache people are informed by their experience in a culturally constituted world of
objects and events with which most of us are unfamiliar. What
sort of world is it? Or, to draw the question into somewhat
sharper focus, what is the cultural context in which Apache
statements such as those presented above find acceptance as
valid claims about reality?

More specifically still, what is required to interpret Annie
Peaches's claim that the land occupied by the Western Apache
is "always stalking people" and that because of this they know
how to "live right?" And how should we understand Chairman
Lupe's assertion that Apache children sometimes misbehave
because the land "doesn't go to work on them any more?" Why
does Nick Thompson claim that his knowledge of placenames
and historical events enables him to "stay away from badness?"
And why does Benson Lewis liken placenames to pictures, stories to arrows, and a mountain near the community at Cibecue
to his maternal grandmother? What should we make of Wilson
Lavender's recollection of an unhappy time in California when
forgetting placenames and stories caused him to forget "how to
be strong?" Are these claims structured in metaphorical terms,
or, given Western Apache assumptions about the physical universe and the place of people within it, are they somehow to be
interpreted literally? In any case, what is the reasoning that lies
behind the claims, the informal logic of which they are simultaneously products and expressions? Above all, what makes the
claims make sense?

I address these and other questions through an investigation of how Western Apaches talk about the natural landscape and the importance they attach to named locations within it. Accordingly, my discussion focuses on elements of language and patterns of speech, my purpose being to discover from these elements and patterns something of how Apache people construe their land and render it intelligible. Whenever Apaches describe the land—or, as happens more frequently, whenever they tell stories about incidents that have occurred at particular points upon it—they take steps to constitute it in relation to themselves. Which is simply to say that in acts of speech, mundane and otherwise, Apaches negotiate images and understandings of the land that are accepted as credible accounts of what it actually is, why it is significant, and how it impinges on the daily lives of men and women. In short, portions of a world view are constructed and made available, and a Western Apache version of the landscape is deepened, amplified, and tacitly affirmed. With words, a massive physical presence is fashioned into a meaningful human universe.

This universe of meanings comprises the cultural context in which the Western Apache texts presented earlier acquire their validity and appropriateness. Consequently, if we are to understand the claims set forth in these statements, portions of that context must be explored and made explicit. We must proceed, in other words, by relating our texts to other aspects of Western Apache thought—in effect, to other texts and other claims—and we must continue doing this, more and more comprehensively, until, finally, it is possible to confront the texts directly and expose the major premises on which they rest. As we shall see, most of these premises are grounded in an unformalized native model of Western Apache storytelling which holds that oral narratives have the power to establish enduring bonds between individuals and features of the natural landscape, and that as a direct consequence of such bonds, persons who have acted improperly will be moved to reflect critically on their misconduct and resolve to improve it. A native model of how stories work to shape Apaches' conceptions of the landscape, it is also a model of how stories work to shape Apaches' conceptions of themselves. Ultimately, it is a model of how two symbolic resources—language and the land—are manipulated by Apaches to promote compliance with standards for acceptable social behavior and the moral values that support them.

Should it appear, then, that these Western Apache texts lack either substance or complexity, we shall see that in fact both qualities are present in ample measure. And should the aim of interpreting such modestly worded documents seem unduly narrow, or my strategy for trying to accomplish it too tightly bound up with an examination of linguistic and ethnographic particulars, it will become evident soon enough that wider and more general issues are very much involved. Of these, I suggest, none is more pressing or conspicuous than the reluctance of cultural ecologists to deal openly and in close detail with the symbolic attributes of human environments and the effects of environmental constructions on patterns of social action.

But I am getting ahead of myself. The problem is how to get started, and for advice on that matter I turn here, as I actually did in Cibecue several years ago, to a gifted and unusual man. Teacher and consultant, serious thinker and salacious joker alike, he has so strongly influenced the content and organization of this essay that he has become, with his permission, a part of it himself—and so, too, of the interpretation it presents.

"Learn the Names"

Nick Thompson is, by his own admission, an old man. It is possible, he told me once, that he was born in 1918. Beneath snow-white hair cut short, his face is round and compact, his features small and sharply molded. His large, black, and very bright eyes move quickly, and when he smiles he acquires an expression that is at once mischievous and intimidating. I have known him for more than twenty years, and he has instructed me often on matters pertaining to Western Apache language and culture. A man who delights in play, he has also teased me unmercifully, concocted humorous stories about me that are thoroughly apocryphal, and embarrassed me before large numbers of incredulous Apaches by inquiring publicly into the most intimate details of my private life. Described by many people in Cibecue as a true 'Slim Coyote' (*ma' ts'ósé*), Nick Thompson

is outspoken, incorrigible, and unabashed.[1] He is also gener-
ous, thoughtful, and highly intelligent. I value his friendship
immensely.

As I bring my Jeep to a halt on the road beside the old man's
camp, I hear Nick complaining loudly to his wife about the
changing character of life in Cibecue and its regrettable effects
on younger members of the community. I have heard these
complaints before and I know they are deeply felt. But still, on
this sunny morning in June 1977, it is hard to suppress a smile,
for the image Nick presents, a striking example of what can be
achieved with sartorial *bricolage,* is hardly what one would expect of a staunch tribal conservative. Crippled since childhood
and partially paralyzed by a recent stroke, the old man is seated
in the shade of a cottonwood tree a few yards from the modest
wooden cabin where he lives with his wife and two small grand-
children. He is smoking a Salem cigarette and is studying with
undisguised approval the shoes on his feet—a new pair of bright
blue Nike running shoes trimmed in incandescent orange. He
is also wearing a pair of faded green trousers, a battered brown
cowboy hat, and a white T-shirt with "Disneyland" printed in
bold red letters across the front. Within easy reach of his chair,
resting on the base of an upended washtub, is a copy of the *National Enquirer,* a mug of hot coffee, and an open box of chocolate-covered doughnuts. If Nick Thompson is an opponent of
social change, it is certainly not evident from his appearance.
But appearances can be deceiving, and Nick, who is an accomplished singer and a medicine man of substantial reputation,
would be the first to point this out.

The old man greets me with his eyes. Nothing is said for a
minute or two, but then we begin to talk, exchanging bits of
local news until enough time has passed for me to politely announce the purpose of my visit. I explain that I am puzzled by
certain statements that Apaches have made about the country
surrounding Cibecue and that I am anxious to know how to
interpret them. To my surprise, Nick does not ask what I have
been told or by whom. He responds instead by swinging out his
arm in a wide arc. "Learn the names," he says. "Learn the

names of all these places." Unprepared for such a firm and un-
equivocal suggestion (it sounds to me like nothing less than an
order), I retreat into silence. "Start with the names," the old
man continues. "I will teach you like before. Come back tomorrow morning." Nodding in agreement, I thank Nick for his
willingness to help and tell him what I will be able to pay him.
He says the wage is fair.

A few minutes later, as I stand to take my leave, Nick's face
breaks suddenly into a broad smile and his eyes begin to dance.
I know that look very well and brace myself for the farewell
joke that almost always accompanies it. The old man wastes no
time. He says I look lonely. He urges me to have prolonged and
abundant sex with very old women. He says it prevents nose-
bleeds. He says that someday I can write a book about it. Flus-
tered and at a loss for words, I smile weakly and shake my head.
Delighted with this reaction, Nick laughs heartily and reaches
for his coffee and a chocolate-covered doughnut.

I return to the old man's camp the following day and start to
learn Western Apache placenames. My lessons, which are interrupted by mapping trips with more mobile Apache consultants,
continue for the next ten weeks. In late August, shortly before
I must leave Cibecue, Nick asks to see the maps. He is not impressed. "White men need paper maps," he observes. "We have
maps in our minds."

Western Apache Placenames

The study of American Indian placename systems has fallen on
hard times. Once a viable component of anthropology in the
United States, it has virtually ceased to exist, the inconspicu-
ous victim of changing intellectual fashions and large amounts
of ethnographic neglect. There are good reasons for advocating
a revival. As early as 1900, Franz Boas, who was deeply impressed by the minutely detailed environmental knowledge of
the Baffin Land and Hudson Bay Eskimo, suggested that one of
the most profitable ways to explore the "mental life" of Indian
peoples was to investigate their geographical nomenclatures
(Boas 1901–07). In 1912, Edward Sapir made the same point in

more general terms, saying that Indian vocabularies provided valuable insight into native conceptions of the natural world and all that was held to be significant within it. Later, in 1934, Boas published a short monograph entitled *Geographical Names of the Kwakiutl Indians*. This essay is essentially a study of Kwakiutl word morphology, but it demonstrates beautifully Boas's earlier ideas concerning the Eskimo: namely, that the study of placename systems may reveal a great deal about the cognitive categories with which environmental phenomena are organized and understood. This tradition of research, which also included J. P. Harrington's (1916) massive treatise on Tewa placenames, began to falter in the years preceding World War II. A few brief articles appeared in the 1950s, and Floyd Lounsbury contributed an important paper on Iroquois placenames in 1960. Since then, however, little work has been done. Indeed, with the notable exception of Frederica de Laguna's (1972) long-delayed monograph on the Tlingit, I know of not a single study written by a linguist or anthropologist in the past twenty years that deals extensively or in depth with the placename system of a North American tribe.[2]

One can only imagine how Boas or Sapir or Harrington might have reacted to Nick Thompson's interest in Western Apache placenames. They would have been intrigued, I think, but probably not surprised. For each of them had come to understand, as I am just beginning to at Cibecue, that American Indian placenames are intricate little creations and that studying their internal structure, together with the functions they serve in spoken conversation, can lead the ethnographer to any number of useful discoveries. All that is required is sound instruction from able native consultants, a fondness for mapping extensive areas of territory, and a modest capacity for wonder and delight at the large tasks that small words can be made to perform. And one more thing: a willingness to reject the widely accepted notion that placenames are nothing more than handy vehicles of reference. Placenames do refer, and quite indispensably at that; but in communities such as Cibecue, they are used and valued for other reasons as well.

Located in a narrow valley at an elevation of 1507 meters, the settlement at Cibecue (from *deeschii' bikoh,* 'valley with elongated red bluffs') is bisected by a shallow stream emanating from springs that rise in low-lying mountains to the north. Apache homes, separated by horse pastures, agricultural plots, and ceremonial dance grounds, are located on both sides of the stream for a distance of approximately 8 kilometers. The valley itself, which is bounded on the east and west by a series of red sandstone bluffs, displays marked topographic diversity in the form of heavily dissected canyons and arroyos, broad alluvial floodplains, and several clusters of prominent peaks. Vegetation ranges from a mixed ponderosa pine-Douglas fir association near the headwaters of Cibecue Creek to a chaparral community, consisting of scrub oak, cat's-claw, agave, and a variety of cactus species, at the confluence of the creek with the Salt River. In between, numerous other floral associations occur, including dense riparian communities and heavy stands of cottonwood, oak, walnut, and pine.

Together with Michael W. Graves, I have mapped nearly 104 square kilometers in and around the community at Cibecue and within this area have recorded the Western Apache names of 296 locations; it is, to say the least, a region densely packed with placenames. But large numbers alone do not account for the high frequency with which placenames typically appear in Western Apache discourse. In part, this pattern of regular and recurrent use results from the fact that Apaches, who travel a great deal to and from their homes, habitually call on each other to describe their trips in detail. Almost invariably, and in sharp contrast to comparable reports delivered by Anglos living at Cibecue, these descriptions focus as much on *where* events occurred as on the nature and consequences of the events themselves. This practice has been observed in other Apachean groups as well, including, as Harry Hoijer (personal communication, 1973) notes, the Navajo: "Even the most minute occurrences are described by Navajos in close conjunction with their physical settings, suggesting that unless narrated events are *spatially anchored* their significance is somehow reduced and cannot be properly assessed." Hoijer could just as well be speaking of the Western Apache.

Something else contributes to the common use of placenames in Western Apache communities, however, and that, quite simply, is that Apaches enjoy using them. Several years ago, for example, when I was stringing a barbed-wire fence with two Apache cowboys from Cibecue, I noticed that one of them was talking quietly to himself. When I listened carefully, I discovered that he was reciting a list of placenames—a long list, punctuated only by spurts of tobacco juice, that went on for nearly ten minutes. Later, when I ventured to ask him about it, he said he "talked names" all the time. Why? "I like to," he said. "I ride that way in my mind." And on dozens of other occasions when I have been working or traveling with Apaches, they have taken satisfaction in pointing out particular locations and pronouncing their names—once, twice, three times or more. Why? "Because we like to," or "Because those names are good to say." More often, however, Apaches account for their enthusiastic use of placenames by commenting on the precision with which the names depict their referents. "That place looks just like its name," someone will explain, or "That name makes me see that place like it really is." Or, as Benson Lewis (text 4) states so succinctly, "It's name is like a picture."

Statements such as these may be interpreted in light of certain facts about the linguistic structure of Western Apache placenames. To begin with, it is essential to understand that all but a very few Apache placenames take the form of complete sentences. This is made possible by one of the most prominent components of the Western Apache language: an elaborate system of prefixes that operates most extensively and productively to modify the stems of verbs. Thus, well-formed sentences can be constructed that are extremely compact yet semantically very rich. It is this combination of brevity and expressiveness, I believe, that appeals to Apaches and makes the mere pronunciation of placenames a satisfying experience.

By way of illustration, consider the pair of placenames shown in examples 6 and 7 below, which have been segmented into their gross morphological constituents.

6. *tsé biká' tú yahiłíí*: *tsé* ('rock', 'stone') + *biká'* ('on top of it'; a flattish object) + *tú* ('water') + *ya-* ('downward') + *-hi-* (linear succession of regularly repeated movements) + *-łíí'* ('it flows').

Gloss: 'water flows down on top of a regular succession of flat rocks'

7. *t'iis bitł'áh tú 'olíí'*: *t'iis* ('cottonwood tree') + *bitł'áh* ('below it', 'underneath it') + *tú* ('water') + *'o-* ('inward') + *-łíí'* ('it flows').

Gloss: 'water flows inward underneath a cottonwood tree'

Notice how thoroughly descriptive these placenames are and how pointedly specific in the physical details they pick out. The two names presented here are not unique in this respect. On the contrary, descriptive specificity is characteristic of most Western Apache placenames, and it is this attribute, almost certainly, that causes Apaches to liken placenames to pictures and to comment appreciatively on the capacity of placenames to evoke full and accurate images of the locations to which they refer.

Further evidence that Western Apaches value descriptive specificity in placenames comes from a distinction that is drawn between 'long names' (*bízhi' ndeez*) and 'shortened names' (*bízhi' 'ígod*). In this connection, it is important to note that most Apache placenames consist minimally of a noun marking the subject, an imperfective neuter verb that functions as an adjectival modifier, and a perfective neuter verb that describes some aspect of the position, posture, or shape of the subject. However, some Apache placenames lack a perfective neuter verb and consist exclusively of a noun and an imperfective adjectival. In my sample of 296 placenames, 247 (83 percent) belong to the former type, while 49 (17 percent) belong to the latter. Examples of both types are given below.

Type 1: Placenames containing a perfective neuter verb

8. *tsé łigai dah sidil*: *tsé* ('rock', 'stone') + *łigai* ('white') + *dah* ('above ground level') + *sidil* ('three or more objects lie in a compact cluster').

Gloss: 'white rocks lie above in a compact cluster'

9. *goshtł'ish tú bił sikáá*: *goshtł'ish* ('mud') + *tú* ('water')

+ *bił* ('in association with') + *sikάά* ('a container with its contents lies').

Gloss: 'muddy water lies in a concave depression'

Type 2: Placenames lacking a perfective neuter verb

10. *nadah nch'íí'*: *nadah* ('mescal') + *nch'íí'* (it is bitter-tasting').

Gloss: 'bitter-tasting mescal'

11. *ch'o'oł ntsaaz*: *ch'o'oł* ('juniper tree') + *ntsaaz* ('it is big and wide').

Gloss: 'big wide juniper tree'

I draw attention to this typological difference among Western Apache placenames because it coincides closely with, and probably provides the grammatical basis for, the 'long' versus 'shortened' distinction that Apaches themselves recognize and comment on. Placenames containing a perfective neuter verb were consistently identified by a group of twelve Apache consultants from Cibecue as belonging to the 'long' category of names, while those lacking a perfective neuter verb were consistently assigned to its 'shortened' counterpart. In addition, and more revealing still, all but one consultant maintained that the 'long names' were "better" than the 'shortened' ones because they "told more" or "said more" about the physical properties of their referents. It seems reasonable to conclude, then, that placenames containing a perfective neuter verb are appreciated by Apaches as being more fully descriptive of their referents than placenames in which a perfective neuter verb is absent. And so, in fact, the former usually are.

Given these observations, it should come as no surprise that the large majority of Western Apache placenames present descriptions of the locations to which they refer. All of the placenames considered so far belong to this dominant type, as do 268 (90 percent) of the 296 names in my sample. Apaches observe, however, that some placenames do not describe their referents and are derived from other sources. These include (1) placenames that allude to activities that were formerly performed at or near the sites in question, (2) placenames that refer to 'dangerous' (*bégódzig*) locations, and (3) placenames that allude to historical events that are known to have occurred at or near the sites they designate. Examples of these three types, together with brief descriptions of their sources, are given here.

Type 3: Placenames alluding to former activities

12. *ndee dah naazį́į́h: ndee* ('man', 'person', 'Apache') + *dah* ('above ground level') + *naazį́į́h* ('three or more animate objects stand about').

Gloss: 'men stand about above'

(This name refers to a point on a low ridge that commands an excellent view of the southern portion of Cibecue Valley. Prior to 1872, Apache men were stationed here as lookouts to guard against surprise attacks from Pimas, Papagos, Navajos, and troops of the U. S. Sixth Cavalry.)

13. *gową dahitą́ą́: gową* ('camp', 'wickiup') + *dahitą́ą́* ('crescent moon'; literally, a slender solid object appears).

Gloss: 'crescent moon camp'

(This is the name of a large meadow where a four-day religious ceremonial called *hádndín 'aldee* ('pollen is placed') was formerly performed. The ritual began with the appearance of the first new moon in April or May. The temporary brush dwellings of the participants were arranged side by side in the shape of a crescent.)

Type 4: Placenames referring to 'dangerous places' (*bégódzig goz'ą́ą́*)

14. *dahzíné sidaa: dahzíné* ('porcupine') + *sidaa* ('an animate object sits').

Gloss: 'a porcupine sits'

(This name refers to the upper end of a large arroyo near the community of Cibecue where porcupines used to gather in early winter. Western Apaches hold that direct contact with porcupines, or with anything contaminated with porcupine urine or feces or hair, may result in serious illness.)

15. *ma' bichan 'o'áá: ma'* ('coyote') + *bichan* ('its feces') + *'o'áá* ('a solid object sticks up').

Gloss: 'a pile of coyote feces sticks up'

(This name designates a large meadow where coyotes congregate to hunt field mice and jackrabbits. Like porcupines, coyotes and their excuviae are regarded by Apaches as a source of sickness.)

Type 5: Placenames alluding to historical events

16. *tá'ke godzig: tá'ke* ('field', 'farm') + *godzig* ('rotten', 'spoiled').

Gloss: 'rotten field'

(This is the name of a small flat where a group of Western Apaches planted corn many years ago. One spring, after the corn had sprouted, the people left their camps nearby to search for mescal in mountains to the south. They returned to discover that all their corn had been killed by a black, foul-smelling blight.)

17. *łį́į́' tę́hitlizh: łį́į́'* ('horse') + *tę́hitlizh* ('it fell down into water').

Gloss: 'horse fell down into water'

(This name refers to a site where a young Apache woman, returning home after gathering mescal, allowed the horse she was riding to walk too close to a rocky ledge above Cibecue Creek. The horse lost its balance and fell with its rider into the stream below. The horse survived; the woman did not.)

Of the 296 Apache placenames in my sample, only 28 (less than 10 percent) were assigned by consultants from Cibecue to the three types exemplified above (Type 3 = 9; Type 4 = 6; Type 5 = 13). This finding would seem to lend added support to the view that Western Apaches favor placenames that provide precise and accurate information about observable features of the natural landscape—and the more information the better.[3]

Why should this be so? The reasons, no doubt, are multiple, but one of them may be closely linked to the stylistic functions served by placenames in Western Apache storytelling. Placenames are used in all forms of Apache storytelling as situating devices, as conventionalized instruments for locating narrated events at and in the physical settings where the events have occurred. Thus, instead of describing these settings discursively, an Apache storyteller can simply employ their names and Apache listeners, whether they have visited the locations or not, are able to imagine in some detail how they might appear. In this way, to borrow Hoijer's felicitous phrase, narrated events are "spatially anchored" at points on the land, and the evocative pictures presented by Western Apache place-names become indispensable resources for the storyteller's craft.

"All These Places Have Stories"

When I return to Cibecue in the spring of 1978, Nick Thompson is recovering from a bad case of the flu. He is weak, despondent, and uncomfortable. We speak very little and no mention is made of placenames. His wife is worried about him and so am I. Within a week, however, Nick's eldest son comes to my camp with a message: I am to visit his father and bring with me two packs of Salem cigarettes and a dozen chocolate-covered doughnuts. This is good news.

When I arrive at the old man's camp, he is sitting under the cottonwood tree by his house. A blanket is draped across his knees and he is wearing a heavy plaid jacket and a red vinyl cap with white fur-lined earflaps. There is color in his cheeks and the sparkle is back in his eyes. Shortly after we start to converse, and a propos of nothing I can discern, Nick announces that in 1931 he had sexual intercourse eight times in one night. He wants to know if I have ever been so fortunate. His wife, who has brought us each a cup of coffee, hears this remark and tells him that he is a crazy old man. Nick laughs loudly. Plainly, he is feeling better.

Eventually, I ask Nick if he is ready to resume our work together. "Yes," he says, "but no more on names." What then? "Stories," is his reply. "All these places have stories. We shoot each other with them, like arrows. Come back tomorrow morning." Puzzled once again, but suspecting that the old man has a plan he wants to follow, I tell him I will return. We then discuss Nick's wages. He insists that I pay him more than I did the year before as it is necessary to keep up with inflation. I agree and we settle on a larger sum. Then comes the predictable farewell joke: a fine piece of nonsense in which Nick, speaking English and imitating certain mannerisms he has come to associate with Anglo physicians, diagnoses my badly sunburned nose as an advanced case of venereal disease.[4] This time it is Nick's wife who laughs loudest.

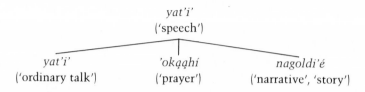

FIGURE 13. Major categories of Western Apache speech.

The next day Nick begins to instruct me on aspects of Western Apache storytelling. Consulting on a regular basis with other Apaches from Cibecue as well, I pursue this topic throughout the summer of 1978.

Historical Tales

If placenames appear frequently in ordinary forms of Western Apache discourse, their use is equally conspicuous in oral narratives. It is here, in conjunction with stories Apaches tell, that we can move closer to an interpretation of native claims about the symbolic importance of geographical features and the personalized relationships that individuals may have with them. As shown in figure 13, the people of Cibecue classify 'speech' (yat'i') into three major forms: 'ordinary talk' (yat'i'), 'prayer' ('okąąhí), and 'narratives' or 'stories' (nagoldi'é). Narratives are further classified into four major and two minor genres (see figure 14). The major genres include 'myths' (godiyįhgo nagoldi'é; literally, 'to tell of holiness'), 'historical tales' ('ágodzaahí or 'ágodzaahí nagoldi'é; literally, 'to tell of that which has happened'), 'sagas' (nlt'éégo nagoldi'é; literally, 'to tell of pleasantness'), and stories that arise in the context of 'gossip' (ch'idii). The minor genres, which do not concern us here, are 'Coyote stories' (ma' highaałyú nagoldi'é; literally, 'to tell of Coyote's travels') and 'seduction tales' (biniíma' nagoldi'é; literally, 'to tell of sexual desires').

Western Apaches distinguish among the major narrative genres on two basic semantic dimensions: time and purpose. Values on the temporal dimension identify in general terms

FIGURE 14. Major categories of Western Apache narrative.

when the events recounted in narratives took place, while values on the purposive dimension describe the objectives that Apache narrators typically have in recounting them (see figure 15). Accordingly, 'myths' deal with events that occurred 'in the beginning' ('godiyaaná'), a time when the universe and all things within it were achieving their present form and location. Performed only by medicine men and medicine women, myths are presented for the primary purpose of enlightenment and instruction: to explain and reaffirm the complex processes by which the known world came into existence. 'Historical tales' recount events that took place 'long ago' (doo'ánííná) when the Western Apache people, having emerged from below the surface of the earth, were developing their own distinctive ways and customs. Most historical tales describe incidents that occurred prior to the coming of the white man, but some of these stories are set in postreservation times, which began for the Western Apache in 1872. Like myths, historical tales are intended to edify, but their main purpose is to alarm and criticize social delinquents (or, as the Apache say, to "shoot" them), thereby impressing such individuals with the undesirability of improper behavior and alerting them to the punitive consequences of further misconduct.

Although sagas deal with historical themes, these narratives are chiefly concerned with events that have taken place in 'modern times' (dííjįįgo), usually within the last sixty or seventy years. In contrast to historical tales, which always focus on serious and disturbing matters, sagas are largely devoid of them. Rather than serving as vehicles of personal criticism, the

NARRATIVE CATEGORY	TEMPORAL LOCUS OF EVENTS	PURPOSES
godiyįhgo nagoldi'é ('myth')	godiyąąná' ('in the beginning')	to enlighten, to instruct
'agodzaahí ('historical tale')	doo'ánííná ('long ago')	to criticize, to warn, to 'shoot'
nłt'éégo nagoldi'é ('saga')	dííjįįgo ('modern times')	to entertain, to engross
ch'idii ('gossip')	k'ad ('now')	to inform to malign

FIGURE 15. Major categories of Western Apache narrative distinguished by temporal locus of events and primary purposes for narration.

primary purpose of sagas is to provide their listeners with relaxation and entertainment. Stories of the kind associated with gossip consist of reports in which persons relate and interpret events involving other members of the Western Apache community. These stories, which embrace incidents that have occurred 'now' or 'at present' (k'ad), are often told for no other reason than to keep people informed of local developments. Not uncommonly, however, narratives in gossip are also used to ridicule and malign the character of their subjects.

Nowhere do placenames serve more important communicative functions than in the context of historical tales. As if to accentuate this fact, stories of the 'ágodzaahí genre are stylistically quite simple. Historical tales require no specialized lexicon, display no unusual syntactical constructions, and involve no irregular morphophonemic alternations; neither are they characterized by unique patterns of stress, pitch, volume, or intonation. In these ways, 'ágodzaahí narratives contrast sharply with myths and sagas, which entail the use of a variety of genre-specific stylistic devices. Historical tales also differ from myths and sagas by virtue of their brevity. Whereas myths and sagas may take hours to complete, historical tales can usually be delivered in less than five minutes. Western Apache storytellers point out that this is both fitting and effective, because *'ágod-zaahí* stories, like the 'arrows' (*k'aa*) they are commonly said to represent, work best when they move swiftly. Finally, and most significant of all, historical tales are distinguished from all other forms of Apache narrative by an opening and closing line that identifies with a placename where the events in the narrative occurred. These lines frame the narrative, mark it unmistakably as belonging to the *'ágodzaahí* genre, and evoke a particular physical setting in which listeners can imaginatively situate everything that happens. It is hardly surprising, then, that while Apache storytellers agree that historical tales are "about" the events recounted in the tales, they also emphasize that the tales are "about" the sites at which the events took place.

If the style of the Western Apache historical tales is relatively unremarkable, their content is just the opposite. Without exception, and usually in very graphic terms, historical tales focus on persons who suffer misfortune as the consequence of actions that violate Apache standards for acceptable social behavior. More specifically, *'ágodzaahí* stories tell of persons who have acted unthinkingly and impulsively in open disregard for 'Apache custom' (*ndee bi 'at'ee'*) and who pay for their transgressions by being humiliated, ostracized, or killed. Stories of the *'ágodzaahí* variety are morality tales pure and simple, and when viewed as such by the Apaches—as compact commentaries on what should be avoided so as to deal successfully and effectively with other people—they are highly informative. For what these narratives assert—tacitly, perhaps, but with dozens of compelling examples—is that immoral behavior is irrevocably a community affair and that persons who behave badly will be punished sooner or later. Thus, just as *'ágodzaahí* stories are "about" historical events and their geographical locations, they are also "about" the system of rules and values according to which Apaches expect each other to organize and regulate their lives. In an even more fundamental sense, then, historical tales are "about" what it means to *be* a Western Apache, or, to make the point less dramatically, what it is that being an Apache should normally and properly entail.

To see how this is so, let us consider the texts of three historical tales and examine the manner in which they have been
interpreted by their Apache narrators.

> 18. It happened at 'big cottonwood trees stand spreading here
> and there'.
>
> Long ago, the Pimas and Apaches were fighting. The Pimas
> were carrying long clubs made from mesquite wood; they were
> also heavy and hard. Before dawn the Pimas arrived at Cibecue
> and attacked the Apaches there. The Pimas attacked while the
> Apaches were still asleep. The Pimas killed the Apaches with
> their clubs. An old woman woke up; she heard the Apaches cry-
> ing out. The old woman thought it was her son-in-law because
> he often picked on her daughter. The old woman cried out:
> "You pick on my child a lot. You should act pleasantly toward
> her." Because the old woman cried out, the Pimas learned
> where she was. The Pimas came running to the old woman's
> camp and killed her with their clubs. A young girl ran away
> from there and hid beneath some bushes. She alone survived.
>
> It happened at 'big cottonwood trees stand spreading here and
> there'.

Narrated by Mrs. Annie Peaches, this historical tale deals
with the harmful consequences that may come to persons who
overstep the traditional role boundaries. During the first year of
marriage it is customary for young Apache couples to live in
the camp of the bride's parents. At this time, the bride's mother
may request that her son-in-law perform different tasks and she
may also instruct and criticize him. Later, however, when the
couple establishes a separate residence, the bride's mother for-
feits this right and may properly interfere in her son-in-law's
affairs only at the request of her daughter. Mrs. Peaches explains that women who do not abide by this arrangement imply
that their sons-in-law are immature and irresponsible, which is
a source of acute embarrassment for the young men and their
wives. Thus, even when meddling might seem to serve a useful
purpose, it should be scrupulously avoided. The woman on
whom this story centers failed to remember this and was instantly killed.

19. It happened at 'coarse-textured rocks lie above in a compact cluster'.

Long ago, a man became sexually attracted to his stepdaughter. He was living below 'coarse-textured rocks lie above in a compact cluster' with his stepdaughter and her mother. Waiting until no one else was present, and sitting alone with her, he started to molest her. The girl's maternal uncle happened to come by and he killed the man with a rock. The man's skull was cracked open. It was raining. The girl's maternal uncle dragged the man's body up above to 'coarse-textured rocks lie above in a compact cluster' and placed it there in a storage pit. The girl's mother came home and was told by her daughter of all that had happened. The people who owned the storage pit removed the man's body and put it somewhere else. The people never had a wake for the dead man's body.

It happened at 'coarse-textured rocks lie above in a compact cluster'.

Narrated by Mr. Benson Lewis, this historical tale deals with the crime of incest, for sexual contact with stepchildren is considered by Western Apaches to be an incestuous act. According to Mr. Lewis, the key line in the story is the penultimate one in which he observes, "The people never had a wake for the dead man's body." We may assume, Mr. Lewis says, that because the dead man's camp was located near the storage pit in which his body was placed, the people who owned the pit were also his relatives. This makes the neglect with which his corpse was treated all the more profound, since kinsmen are bound by the strongest of obligations to care for each other when they die. That the dead man's relatives chose to dispense with customary mortuary ritual shows with devastating clarity that they wished to disown him completely.

20. It happened at 'men stand above here and there'.

Long ago, a man killed a cow off the reservation. The cow belonged to a Whiteman. The man was arrested by a policeman living at Cibecue at 'men stand above here and there'. The policeman was an Apache. The policeman took the man to the head Army officer at Fort Apache. There, at Fort Apache, the head Army officer questioned him. "What do you want?" he said. The policeman said, "I need cartridges and food." The policeman said nothing about the man who had killed the Whiteman's cow. That night some people spoke to the policeman. "It is best to report on him," they said to him. The next day the policeman returned to the head Army officer. "Now what do you want?" he said. The policeman said, "Yesterday I was going to say HELLO and GOOD-BYE but I forgot to do it." Again he said nothing about the man he arrested. Someone was working with words on his mind. The policeman returned with the man to Cibecue. He released him at 'men stand above here and there'.

It happened at 'men stand above here and there'.

This story, narrated by Nick Thompson, describes what happened to an Apache who acted too much like a white man. Between 1872 and 1895, when the Western Apache were strictly confined to their reservations by U.S. military forces, disease and malnutrition took the lives of many people. Consequently, Apaches who listen to this historical tale find it perfectly acceptable that the man who lived at 'men stand above here and there' should have killed and butchered a white man's cow. What is not acceptable is that the policeman, another Apache from the same settlement, should have arrested the rustler and contemplated taking him to jail. But the policeman's plans were thwarted. Someone used witchcraft on him and made him stupid and forgetful. He never informed the military officer at Fort Apache of the real purpose of his visit, and his second encounter with the officer—in which he apologized for neglecting to say hello and good-bye the previous day—revealed him to be an absurd and laughable figure. Although Western Apaches find portions of this story amusing, Nick Thompson explains that they understand it first and foremost as a harsh indictment of persons who join with outsiders against members of their own community and who, as if to flaunt their lack of allegiance, parade the attitudes and mannerisms of white men.

Thus far, my remarks on what Western Apache historical

tales are "about" have centered on features of textual content. This is a familiar strategy and certainly a necessary one, but it is also incomplete. In addition to everything else—places, events, moral standards, conceptions of cultural identity— every historical tale is also "about" the person at whom it is directed. This is because the telling of a historical tale is always prompted by an individual having committed one or more so- cial offenses to which the act of narration, together with the tale itself, is intended as a critical and remedial response. Thus, on those occasions when 'ágodzaahí stories are actually told—by real Apache storytellers, in real interpersonal con- texts, to real social offenders—these narratives are understood to be accompanied by an unstated message from the storyteller that may be phrased something like this: "I know that you have acted in a way similar or analogous to the way in which some- one acted in the story I am telling you. If you continue to act in this way, something similar or analogous to what has happened to the character in the story might also happen to you." This metacommunicative message is just as important as any con- veyed by the text of the storyteller's tale, for Apaches contend that if the message is taken to heart by the person at whom the tale is aimed—and if, in conjunction with lessons drawn from the tale itself, he or she resolves to improve his or her behav- ior—a lasting bond will have been created between that indi- vidual and the site or sites at which events in the tale took place. The cultural premises that inform this powerful idea will be made explicit presently; but first, in order to understand more clearly what the idea involves, let us examine the circum- stances that led to the telling of a historical tale at Cibecue and see how this narrative affected the person for whom it was told.

In early June 1977, a seventeen-year-old Apache woman at- tended a girls' puberty ceremonial at Cibecue with her hair rolled up in a set of pink plastic curlers. She had returned home two days before from a boarding school in Utah where this sort of ornamentation was considered fashionable by her peers. Something so mundane would have gone unnoticed by others were it not for the fact that Western Apache women of all ages are expected to appear at puberty ceremonials with their hair worn loose. This is one of several ways that women have of showing respect for the ceremonial and also, by implication, for the people who have staged it. The practice of presenting oneself with free-flowing hair is also understood to contribute to the ceremonial's effectiveness, for Apaches hold that the ritual's most basic objectives, which are to invest the pubescent girl with qualities necessary for life as an adult, cannot be achieved unless standard forms of respect are faithfully observed. On this occasion at Cibecue, everyone was following custom except the young woman who arrived wearing curlers. She soon became an object of attention and quiet expressions of disapproval, but no one spoke to her about the cylindrical objects in her hair.

Two weeks later, the same young woman made a large stack of tortillas and brought them to the camp of her maternal grandmother, a widow in her mid-sixties who had organized a small party to celebrate her eldest grandson's birthday. Eighteen people were on hand, myself included, and all of us were treated to hot coffee and a dinner of boiled beef and potatoes. When the meal was over casual conversation began to flow, and the young woman seated herself on the ground next to her younger sister. And then—quietly, deftly, and totally without warning—her grandmother narrated a version of the historical tale about the forgetful Apache policeman who behaved too much like a white man. Shortly after the story was finished, the young woman stood up, turned away wordlessly, and walked off in the direction of her home. Uncertain of what had happened, I asked her grandmother why she had departed. Had the young woman suddenly become ill? "No," her grandmother replied. "I shot her with an arrow."

Approximately two years after this incident occurred, I found myself in the company of the young woman with the taste for distinctive hairstyles. She had purchased a large carton of groceries at the trading post at Cibecue, and when I offered to drive her home with them she accepted. I inquired on the way if she remembered the time that her grandmother had told us the story about the forgetful policeman. She said she did and then went on, speaking in English, to describe her reactions to it. "I think maybe my grandmother was getting after me, but then I think maybe not, maybe she's working on somebody else. Then I think back on that dance and I know it's me for sure. I sure don't like how she's talking about me, so I quit looking like that. I threw those curlers away." In order to reach the young woman's camp, we had to pass within a few hundred yards of *ndee dah naazííh* ('men stand above here and there'), the place where the man had lived who was arrested for rustling in the story. I pointed it out to my companion. She said nothing for several moments. Then she smiled and spoke softly in her own language: "I know that place. It stalks me every day."

The comments of this Western Apache woman on her experience as the target of a historical tale are instructive in several respects. To begin with, her statement enables us to imagine something of the sizable psychological impact that historical tales may have on the persons to whom they are presented. Then, too, we can see how *'ágodzaahí* stories may produce quick and palpable effects on the behavior of such individuals, causing them to modify their social conduct in quite specific ways. Lastly, and most revealing of all, the young woman's remarks provide a clear illustration of what Apaches have in mind when they assert that historical tales may establish highly meaningful relationships between individuals and features of the natural landscape.

To appreciate fully the significance of these relationships, as well as their influence on the lives of Western Apache people, we must explore more thoroughly the manner in which the relationships are conceptualized. This can be accomplished through a closer examination of Apache ideas about the activity of storytelling and the acknowledged power of oral narratives, especially historical tales, to promote beneficial changes in people's attitudes toward their responsibilities as members of a moral community. These ideas, which combine to form a native model of how oral narratives work to achieve their intended effects, are expressed in terms of a single dominant metaphor. By now it should come as no surprise to learn that the metaphor draws heavily on the imagery of hunting.

"Stalking with Stories"

Nick Thompson is tired. We have been talking about hunting
with stories for two days now and the old man has not had an
easy time of it. Yesterday, my uneven control of the Western
Apache language prevented him from speaking as rapidly and
eloquently as he would have liked, and on too many occasions
I was forced to interrupt him with questions. At one point,
bored and annoyed with my queries, he told me that I reminded
him of a horsefly buzzing around his head. Later, however,
when he seemed satisfied that I could follow at least the outline
of his thoughts, he recorded on tape a lengthy statement which
he said contained everything he wanted me to know. "Take it
with you and listen to it," he said. "Tomorrow we put it in English." For the past six hours that is what we have been trying
to do. We are finished now and weary of talking. In the weeks
to come I will worry about the depth and force of our translation, and twice more I will return to Nick's camp with other
questions. But the hardest work is over and both of us know it.
Nick has taught me already that hunting with stories is not a
simple matter, and as I prepare to leave I say so. "We know," he
says, and that is all. Here is Nick Thompson's statement:

This is what we know about our stories. They go to work on
your mind and make you think about your life. Maybe you've
not been acting right. Maybe you've been stingy. Maybe you've
been chasing after women. Maybe you've been trying to act like
a Whiteman. People don't *like* it! So someone goes hunting for
you—maybe your grandmother, your grandfather, your uncle. It
doesn't matter. Anyone can do it.

So someone stalks you and tells a story about what happened
long ago. It doesn't matter if other people are around—you're
going to know he's aiming that story at you. All of a sudden it
hits you! It's like an arrow, they say. Sometimes it just bounces
off—it's too soft and you don't think about anything. But when
it's strong it goes in *deep* and starts working on your mind right
away. No one says anything to you, only that story is all, but
now you know that people have been watching you and talking

about you. They don't like how you've been acting. So you have
to think about your life.

Then you feel weak, real weak, like you are sick. You don't
want to eat or talk to anyone. That story is working on you now.
You keep thinking about it. That story is changing you now,
making you want to live right. That story is making you want
to replace yourself. You think only of what you did that was
wrong and you don't like it. So you want to live better. After a
while, you don't like to think of what you did wrong. So you try
to forget that story. You try to pull that arrow out. You think it
won't hurt anymore because now you want to live right.

It's hard to keep on living right. Many things jump up at you
and block your way. But you won't forget that story. You're going to see the place where it happened, maybe every day if it's
nearby and close to Cibecue. If you don't see it, you're going to
hear its name and see it in your mind. It doesn't matter if you
get old—that place will keep on stalking you like the one who
shot you with the story. Maybe that person will die. Even so,
that place will keep on stalking you. It's like that person is still
alive.

Even if we go far away from here to some big city, places
around here keep stalking us. If you live wrong, you will hear
the names and see the places in your mind. They keep on stalking you, even if you go across oceans. The names of all these
places are good. They make you remember how to live right, so
you want to replace yourself again.

A Western Apache Hunting Metaphor

Nick Thompson's model of Western Apache storytelling is a
compelling construction. To be sure, it is the formulation of
one Apache only; but it is fully explicit and amply detailed, and
I have been able to corroborate almost every aspect of it with
other Apaches from Cibecue. This is not to imply that all
Apache people interpret their hunting metaphor for storytelling
in exactly the same fashion. On the contrary, one of the properties of any successful metaphor is that it can be refined and
enlarged in different ways. Thus, some Apaches assert that historical tales, like arrows, leave wounds—mental and emotional

ones—and that the process of "replacing oneself" (a striking concept, that one) is properly understood as a form of healing. Other Apache consultants stress that placenames, rather than the sites to which the names refer, are what individuals are unable to forget after historical tales have done their primary work. But differences and elaborations of this kind only demonstrate the scope and flexibility of the hunting metaphor and do nothing to alter its basic contours or to diminish its considerable force. Neither does such variation reduce in any way the utility of the metaphor as an effective instrument of Western Apache thought.

Although I cannot claim to understand the full range of meanings that the hunting model for storytelling has for Western Apache people, the general premises on which the model rests seem clear to me. Historical tales have the capacity to thrust socially delinquent persons into periods of intense critical self-examination from which (ideally, at least) they emerge chastened, repentant, and determined to "live right." Simultaneously, people who have been "shot" with stories experience a form of anguish—shame, guilt, perhaps only pervasive chagrin—that moves them to alter aspects of their behavior so as to conform more closely to community expectations. In short, historical tales have the power to change people's ideas about themselves: to force them to admit to social failings, to dwell seriously on the significance of these lapses, and to resolve, hopefully once and for all, not to repeat them. As Nick Thompson says, historical tales "make you think about your life."

After stories and storytellers have served this beneficial purpose, features of the physical landscape take over and perpetuate it. Mountains and arroyos step in symbolically for grandmothers and uncles. Just as the latter have "stalked" delinquent individuals in the past, so too particular locations continue to "stalk" them in the present. Such surveillance is essential, Apaches maintain, because "living right" requires constant care and attention, and there is always a possibility that old stories and their initial impact, like old arrows and their wounds, will fade and disappear. In other words, there is always a chance that persons who have "replaced themselves" once—

or twice, or three times—will relax their guard against "bad-ness" and slip back into undesirable forms of social conduct. Consequently, Apaches explain, individuals need to be continu-ously reminded of why they were "shot" in the first place and how they reacted to it at the time. Geographical sites, together with the crisp mental "pictures" of them presented by their names, serve admirably in this capacity, inviting people to re-call their earlier failings and encouraging them to resolve, once again, to avoid them in the future. Grandmothers and uncles must perish but the landscape endures, and for this the Apache people are deeply grateful. "The land," Nick Thompson ob-serves, "looks after us. The land keeps badness away."

It should now be possible for the reader to interpret the West-ern Apache texts at the beginning of this essay in a manner roughly compatible with the Apache ideas that have shaped them. Moreover, he or she should be able to appreciate that the claims put forward in the texts are reasonable and appropriate, culturally credible and "correct," the principled expressions of an underlying logic that invests them with internal consistency and coherent conceptual structure. As we have seen, this struc-ture is supplied in large part by the hunting metaphor for West-ern Apache storytelling. It is chiefly in accordance with this metaphor—or, more exactly, in accordance with the symbolic associations it orders and makes explicit—that the claims pre-sented earlier finally make sense.

Thus, the claim of Annie Peaches—that the land occupied by the Western Apache "makes the people live right"—becomes understandable as a proposition about the moral significance of geographical locations as this has been established by historical tales with which the locations are associated. Similarly, Wilson Lavender's claim—that Apaches who fail to remember place-names "forget how to be strong"—rests on an association of placenames with a belief in the power of historical tales to dis-courage forms of socially unacceptable behavior. Apaches also associate places and their names with the narrators of historical tales, and Benson Lewis's claim—that a certain mountain near Cibecue is his maternal grandmother—can only be interpreted in light of this assumption. The hunting metaphor for storytelling also informs Ronnie Lupe's claim that Western Apache children who are not exposed to historical tales tend to have interpersonal difficulties. As he puts it, "They don't know the stories of what happened at these places. That's why some of them get into trouble." What Mr. Lupe is claiming, of course, is that children who do not learn to associate places and their names with historical tales cannot appreciate the utility of these narratives as guidelines for dealing responsibly and amicably with other people. Consequently, he believes, such individuals are more likely than others to act in ways that run counter to Apache social norms, a sure sign that they are "losing the land."

Losing the land is something the Western Apache can ill afford to do, for geographical features have served the people for centuries as indispensable mnemonic pegs on which to hang the moral teachings of their history. Accordingly, such locations present themselves as instances of what Mikhail Bakhtin calls *chronotopes.* As Bakhtin (1981:7) describes them, chronotopes are

> points in the geography of a community where time and space intersect and fuse. Time takes on flesh and becomes visible for human contemplation; likewise, space becomes charged and responsive to the movements of time and history and the enduring character of a people. . . . Chronotopes thus stand as monuments to the community itself, as symbols of it, as forces operating to shape its members' images of themselves.

Whether one is pleased with Bakhtin's use of the term *chronotope* (it is more widely known, but in a very different sense, as a concept in Einstein's theory of relativity), his observations on the cultural importance of geographical landmarks apply nicely to the Western Apache. The Apache landscape is full of named locations where time and space have fused and where, through the agency of historical tales, their intersection is "made visible for human contemplation." It is also apparent that such locations, charged as they are with personal and social significance, work in important ways to shape the images that Apaches have—or should have—of themselves. Speaking to people like

Nick Thompson and Ronnie Lupe, to Annie Peaches and Benson Lewis, one forms the impression that Apaches view the landscape as a repository of distilled wisdom, a stern but benevolent keeper of tradition, an ever-vigilant ally in the efforts of individuals and whole communities to put into practice a set of standards for social living that are uniquely and distinctively their own. In the world that the Western Apache have constituted for themselves, features of the landscape have become symbols of and for this way of living, the symbols of a culture and the enduring moral character of its people.

We may assume that this relationship with the land has been pervasive throughout Western Apache history; but in today's climate of social change, its importance for Apache people may well be deepening. Communities such as Cibecue, formerly isolated and very much turned inward, were opened up by paved roads less than twenty years ago, and the consequences of improved access and freer travel—including, most noticeably, greatly increased contact with Anglo-Americans—have been pronounced. Younger Apaches, who today complain frequently about the tedium of village life, have started to develop new tastes and ambitions, and some of them are eager to explore the outside world. Older members of the community understand this desire and do little to try to stifle it, but they are concerned that as younger people learn more and more of the "Whiteman's way" they will also lose sight of portions of their own. Let the pink plastic curlers at the girls' puberty ceremonial stand as a case in point. What can be done to guard against this unsettling possibility? Perhaps, in the long run, nothing. But for now, and probably for some time to come, the landscape is doing a respectable job. It is there, "stalking" people all the time, and to the extent that it remains not merely a physical presence but an omnipresent moral force, young Apaches are not likely to forget that the "Whiteman's way" belongs to a different world.

Having pursued Western Apache ideas about the land this far, it is worth inquiring if similar conceptions are held by other groups of American Indian people. Although ethnographic materials bearing on this question are in short supply (I identify some of the reasons for this shortage further on), there is highly reliable evidence from another source—the published work of modern Indian writers—that general similarities do exist. Consider, for example, the following statement by Leslie M. Silko, poet and novelist from the pueblo of Laguna in New Mexico. After explaining that stories "function basically as makers of our identity," Silko (1981:69) goes on to discuss Pueblo narratives in relation to the land:

> The stories cannot be separated from geographical locations, from actual physical places within the land. . . . And the stories are so much a part of these places that it is almost impossible for future generations to lose the stories because there are so many imposing geological elements . . . you cannot *live* in that land without asking or looking at or noticing a boulder or rock. And there's always a story.

A number of other American Indian authors, among them Vine Deloria, Jr. (Sioux), Simon Ortiz (Acoma), Joy Harjo (Creek), and the cultural anthropologist Alfonso Ortiz (San Juan), have written with skill and insight about the moral dimensions of Native American conceptions of the land. No one, however, has addressed the subject with greater sensitivity than N. Scott Momaday (Kiowa). The following passages, taken from his short essay entitled "Native American Attitudes to the Environment" (1974), show clearly what is involved, not only for the Western Apache but for other tribes as well.

> You cannot understand how the Indian thinks of himself in relation to the world around him unless you understand his conception of what is appropriate; particularly what is morally appropriate within the context of that relationship [1974:82].

> The native American ethic with respect to the physical world is a matter of reciprocal appropriation: appropriations in which man invests himself in the landscape, and at the same time incorporates the landscape into his own most fundamental experience. . . . This appropriation is primarily a matter of imagination which is moral in kind. I mean to say that we are all, I suppose, what we imagine ourselves to be. And that is certainly

true of the American Indian. . . . [The Indian] is someone who
thinks of himself in a particular way and his idea comprehends
his relationship to the physical world. He imagines himself
in terms of that relationship and others. And it is that act of
imagination, that moral act of imagination, which constitutes
his understanding of the physical world [1974:80].

"Goodness Is All Around"

The news sweeps through Cibecue like brush fire: Nick
Thompson must have purchased a wheelchair because he was
seen this morning *racing* in one, against his four-year-old
grandson. The little boy, shrieking with glee and running as fast
as he could, won the contest, but the old man finished close
behind. Nick's wife was horrified and his oldest daughter (you
know, the one who hardly ever raises her voice) yelled twice to
him to stop. But he kept on going, wheeling himself along with
his one good arm and paying no attention whatsoever. That old
man will do anything! He doesn't care at all what people think!
And what if he *crashed!*

Nick Thompson has no intention of crashing. Seated now in
his familiar place beneath the cottonwood tree near his house,
he says that racing his wheelchair is perfectly safe. He says he
plans to do it again; he has already challenged his six-year-old
granddaughter. He says he is tired of the women in his camp
telling him what to do. He is also tired of not being able to move
around freely, which is why he bought the wheelchair in the
first place, and people should understand this and stop making
such a fuss. And besides, the old man observes, the wheelchair
has good brakes. That's what he likes best—getting up some
real speed and jamming on the brakes.

The summer of 1980 is almost gone and soon I must leave
Cibecue. I have walked to Nick's camp to tell him good-bye.
This is never easy for me, and we spend most of the time talking
about other things. Eventually, I move to thank him for his gen-
erosity, his patience, and the things he has taught me. Nick responds by pointing with his lips to a low ridge that runs behind
his home in an easterly direction away from Cibecue Creek.

a good place," he says. "These are all good places.
s is all around."

ld man pauses. Then he reaches beneath the seat of his
cha.. nd produces a blue and white cap which he places,
slightly askew, on his head. The embossed emblem in front,
which is in the shape of a car, reads "Ford Racing Team." We
both begin to laugh . . . and laugh and laugh.

Language and Environment

Anthropologists have long been interested in the relationships
that link American Indian communities to their ecological
settings. In the great majority of cases, however, these relationships have been described and interpreted exclusively in materialist terms, that is, in terms of demographic patterns, subsistence strategies, and forms of social organization that facilitate
the exploitation of environmental resources and function in
this way to assure the biological survival of native populations.
While this approach is useful for certain purposes, it is clear
nonetheless that materialist models are one sided and incomplete. Such models ignore the fact that American Indians, like
groups of people everywhere, maintain a complex array of symbolic relationships with their physical surroundings, and that
these relationships, which may have little to do with the serious business of making a living, play a fundamental role in
shaping other forms of social activity. What have been ignored,
in other words, are the cultural instruments with which American Indians fashion understandings of their environments, the
ideational resources with which they constitute their surroundings and invest them with value and significance. We need not
go far to seek the reasons for this neglect. Having committed
themselves to a search for statistical regularities and functional
interdependencies, human ecologists are obliged to regard the
semiotic dimensions of human environments as epiphenomena
that lie outside the proper sphere of their concern. And so,
ironically enough, many human ecologists have become largely
disinterested in what human beings take their environments to
mean. This is unfortunate because, as Csikszentmihalyi and
Rochberg-Halton (1981 : 1) have written,

to understand what people are and what they might become, one must understand what goes on between people and things. What things are cherished, and why, should become part of our knowledge of human beings. Yet it is surprising how little we know about what things mean to people. By and large social scientists have neglected a full investigation of the relationship between people and objects.

There is no doubt in the minds of many anthropologists, including a substantial number who have worked with American Indians, that studies in ecology have made a valuable contribution. In particular, these investigations have shown that indigenous populations may adapt with exquisite intricacy to the physical conditions of their existence (including, of course, the presence of other human populations), and that modifications in these conditions may have a range of dynamic effects on the structure and organization of social institutions. But the fact remains that ecological models have been consistently formulated at a "systemic" level of abstraction that is well removed from the level of the individual—and it is individuals, not social institutions, who make and act on cultural meanings. Conventional ecological studies proceed on the tacit premise that what people think about the environment—how they perceive it, conceptualize it, or, to borrow a phrase from the ethnomethodologists, "actively construct" it—is basically irrelevant to an understanding of man-land relationships. If this premise is accepted as correct, we must conclude that cultural meanings are similarly irrelevant and that the layers of significance with which human beings blanket the environment have little bearing on how they lead their lives. But the premise is not correct, for American Indians or anyone else, and to suppose otherwise would be a serious mistake.

Accordingly, and by way of illustration, I have attempted to show here that Western Apache conceptions of the land work in specific ways to influence Apaches' conceptions of themselves (and vice versa), and that the two together work to influence patterns of social action. To reject this possibility—or, as many ecologists would be inclined to do, to rule it out a priori as inconsequential—would have the effect of "removing" the Apache from the world as they have constructed it. This, in turn, would obliterate all aspects of their moral relationship with the land. For reasons that should now be apparent, this relationship is crucial to Apaches—quite as crucial, I expect, as any that deals with subsistence or economics—and for us to lose sight of it could only have damaging consequences.

Societies must survive, but social life is more than just surviving. And cultural meanings are epiphenomenal only for those who choose to make them so. I would like to witness the development of a cultural ecology that is cultural in the fullest sense, a broader and more flexible approach to the study of man-land relationships in which the symbolic properties of environmental phenomena receive the same kind of care and attention that has traditionally been given to their material counterparts. The Western Apache of Cibecue understand their land, and act on their understandings of it, in ways that standard ecological approaches would overlook. Does this mean that such understandings are unimportant for the Western Apache? For a stronger and more rounded anthropology? I suggest that on both counts it does not.

Cultural constructions of the environment, whether those of American Indians or of peoples elsewhere in the world, will remain largely inaccessible unless we are prepared to sit down and listen to our native consultants talk—not only about landscapes, which of course we must do, but about talking about landscapes as well. And since spatial conceptions, like temporal ones, are so often found expressed in figurative language, this is almost certain to lead to a consideration of metaphor. Paul Radin (1916 : 137), writing some years ago of the Winnebago Indians of the Great Lakes, described a particular case that is probably typical of many others:

> Ideas about the habitat are frequently set forth in elaborate similes and metaphors which equate disparate objects in a fashion that at first seems quite unfathomable. Yet once these tropes are uncovered, it can be seen that they rest upon firm assumptions about the workings of nature which, though different from our own, fit together intelligibly.

George Lakoff and Mark Johnson (1980:1) have recently stated that the essence of metaphor is "understanding and experiencing one kind of thing in terms of another." Although this definition departs relatively little from the classical one given by Aristotle ("metaphor implies an intuitive perception of the similarity in dissimilars"), it points to a problem in the study of language and culture that is deeply ethnographic. For where metaphor is concerned, the question always arises, On what *grounds* is one kind of thing understood in terms of another? In other words, what must individuals believe about themselves and their surroundings for their metaphors to "work?"

This question focuses attention on the large body of implicit cultural assumptions that the members of any speech community rely on to interpret instances of situated discourse. Such assumptions, which have been variously described as comprising a speaker's "presuppositions," "background knowledge," or "beliefs about the world," present difficulties for all theories of language that seek to restrict the idea of linguistic competence to a speaker's tacit knowledge of grammatical rules. Metaphor threatens both the validity of this distinction and the utility of maintaining it, because the ability to interpret even the simplest forms of metaphorical speech cannot be accounted for with grammatical rules alone; presuppositions are also fundamentally involved. This is clearly illustrated by Nick Thompson's statement on the Western Apache hunting metaphor for storytelling. As he explicates the metaphor, thereby enabling us to interpret a set of claims that Apaches have made, he articulates the cultural assumptions that make these claims possible in the first place. In other words, he makes presuppositions explicit. Storytellers are hunters for the Western Apache—and stories, arrows; and mountains, grandmothers—by virtue of shared beliefs about the world. Culturally wrought and culturally specific, such beliefs provide the conceptual materials with which competent Apache speakers locate the similarities in metaphorical dissimilars and, in so doing, experience one kind of thing in terms of another. Such beliefs make their metaphors "work."

What all of this implies (obviously for many anthropologists, less so for many linguists) is that grasping other peoples' metaphors requires ethnography as much as it does linguistics. Unless we pursue the two together, the full extent to which metaphorical structures influence patterns of thought and action is likely to elude us. "To inhabit a language," Samuel Johnson wrote, "is to inhabit a living universe, and vice-versa." That "vice versa" is critical because it suggests, correctly I believe, that linguistics and ethnography are integral parts of the same basic enterprise, one of whose purposes is to construct principled interpretations of culturally constituted worlds and to try to understand what living in them is like. I am not certain where the theoretical line between language and culture should be drawn; there are times when I wonder if it can be sharply drawn at all. But this much seems reasonably clear: if anthropology stands to benefit from an approach to cultural ecology that attends more closely to the symbolic forms with which human environments are perceived and rendered significant, so, too, there is a need for an expanded view of linguistic competence in which beliefs about the world occupy a central place. If it is the meaning of things that we are after—the meanings of words, objects, events, and the claims people make about themselves—language and culture must be studied hand in hand. Our knowledge of one can only enhance our knowledge of the other.

"We Know It Happened"

If the thoughts presented here have a measure of theoretical interest, recent experience persuades me that they can have practical value as well. In recent years I have authored a number of documents for use in litigation concerning the settlement of Western Apache water rights in Arizona. Until a final decision is reached in the case, I am not permitted to describe the contents of these documents in detail, but one of my assignments has been to write a report dealing with Apache conceptions of the physical environment. That report contains sections on Western Apache placenames, oral narratives, and certain metaphors that Apaches use to formulate aspects of their relationship with the land.

Preliminary hearings resulted in a judgment favorable to Apache interests, and apparently my report was useful, mainly because it helped to pave the way for testimony by native witnesses. One of these witnesses was Nick Thompson, and according to attorneys on both sides, the old man's appearance had a decisive impact. After Nick had taken his place on the stand, he was asked by an attorney why he considered water to be important to his people. A man of eminent good sense, Nick replied, "Because we drink it!" And then, without missing a beat, he launched into a historical tale about a large spring not far from Cibecue—*tú nchaa halį́į́'* ('lots of water flows up and out')—where long ago a man was mysteriously drowned after badly mistreating his wife. When Nick finished the story he went on to say: "We know it happened, so we know not to act like that man who died. It's good we have that water. We need it to live. It's good we have that spring too. We need it to live right." Then the old man smiled to himself and his eyes began to dance.

7 / 'Speaking with Names': Language and Landscape Among the Western Apache

What we call the landscape is generally considered to be something "out there." But, while some aspects of the landscape are clearly external to both our bodies and our minds, what each of us actually experiences is selected, shaped, and colored by what we know.

BARRIE GREENBIE

An unfamiliar landscape, like an unfamiliar language, is always a little daunting, and when the two are encountered together—as they are, commonly enough, in those out-of-the-way communities where ethnographers have a tendency to crop up—the combination may be downright unsettling. From the outset, of course, neither landscape nor language can be ignored. On the contrary, the shapes and colors and contours of the land, together with the shifting sounds and cadences of native discourse, thrust themselves upon the newcomer with a force so vivid and direct as to be virtually inescapable. Yet for all their sensory immediacy (and there are occasions, as any ethnographer will attest, when the sheer constancy of it grows to formidable proportions) landscape and discourse seem resolutely out of reach. Although close at hand and tangible in the extreme, each in its own way appears remote and inaccessible, anonymous and indistinct, and somehow, implausibly, a shade less than fully believable. And neither one, as if determined to accentuate these conflicting impressions, may seem the least bit interested in having them resolved. Emphatically "there" but conspicuously lacking in accustomed forms of order and arrangement, landscape and discourse confound the stranger's efforts to invest them with significance, and this uncommon predicament, which produces nothing if not uncertainty, can be keenly disconcerting.

Surrounded by foreign geographical objects and intractable acts of speech, even the most practiced ethnographers become diffident and cautious, for the meanings of objects and acts alike can only be guessed at, and once the guesses have been recognized for the arbitrary constructions they almost always are, one senses acutely that one's own experience of things and events "out there" cannot be used as a reliable guide to the experience of native people. In other words, one must acknowledge that local understandings of external realities are ineluctably fashioned from local cultural materials, and that, knowing little or nothing of the latter, one's ability to make appropriate sense of "what is" and "what occurs" in one's environment is bound to be deficient. For better or worse, the ethnographer sees, landscape and speech acts do not interpret their own significance. Initially at least, and typically for many months to come, this is a task that only members of the indigenous community are adequately equipped to accomplish; and accomplish it they do, day in and day out, with enviably little difficulty. For where native men and women are concerned the external world *is* as it appears to them to be—naturally, unproblematically, and more or less consistently—and rarely do they have reason to consider that the coherence it displays is an intricate product of their own collective manufacture. Cultures run deep, as the saying goes, and natives everywhere take their "natives' point of view" very much for granted.

In this way (or something roughly like it) the ethnographer comes to appreciate that features of the local landscape, no less than utterances exchanged in forms of daily discourse, acquire value and significance by virtue of the ideational systems with which they are apprehended and construed. Symbolically constituted, socially transmitted, and individually applied, such systems operate to place flexible constraints on how the physical environment can (and should) be known, how its occupants can (and should) be found to act, and how the doings of both can (and should) be discerned to affect each other. Accordingly, each system delineates a distinctive way of being-in-the-world (Ricoeur 1979), an informal logic for engaging the world and thinking about the engagement (Geertz 1973), an array of conceptual frameworks for organizing experience and rendering it intelligible (Goffman 1974). In any community, the meanings assigned to geographical features and acts of speech will be influenced by the subjective determinations of the people who assign them, and these determinations, needless to say, will exhibit variation. But the character of the meanings—their steadier themes, their recurrent tonalities, and, above all, their conventionalized modes of expression—will bear the stamp of a common cast of mind. Constructions of reality that reflect conceptions of reality itself, the meanings of landscapes and acts of speech are personalized manifestations of a shared perspective on the human condition.

Mulling over these apparent truths, the ethnographer is likely to notice that members of the local community involve themselves with their geographical landscape in at least three distinct ways. First, they may simply observe the landscape, attending for reasons of their own to aspects of its appearance and to sundry goings-on within it. Second, they may utilize the landscape, engaging in a broad range of physical activities that, depending on their duration and extent, may leave portions of the landscape visibly modified. Third, native people may communicate about the landscape, formulating descriptions and other representations of it that they share in the course of social gatherings. On many occasions, community members can be observed to alternate freely among these different modes of involvement (they may also, of course, combine them), but it is obvious that events in the latter mode—communicative acts of topographic representation—will be most revealing of the conceptual instruments with which native people interpret their natural surroundings. And although such representations may be fashioned from a variety of semiotic materials (gestural, pictorial, musical, and others), it is equally plain that few will be more instructive in this regard than those that are wrought with words.

Ordinary talk, the ethnographer sees, provides a readily available window onto the structure and significance of other peoples' worlds, and so (slowly at first, by fits and starts, and never without protracted bouts of guessing) he or she begins to learn to listen. And also to freshly see. For as native concepts and beliefs find external purchase on specific features of the local topography, the entire landscape seems to acquire a crisp new dimension that moves it more surely into view. What earlier appeared as a circular sweep of undifferentiated natural architecture now starts to emerge as a precise arrangement of named sites and localities, each of which is distinguished by a set of physical attributes and cultural associations that marks it as unique. In native discourse, the local landscape falls neatly and repeatedly into *places*—and places, as Franz Boas (1934) emphasized some years ago, are social constructions par excellence.

It is excessive to claim, as George Trager (1968:537) has done, that "the way man talks about the physical universe is his only way of knowing anything about it." Nonetheless, most ethnographers would agree that Trager's claim contains a substantial amount of truth, and some have suggested that this can be seen with particular clarity where language and landscapes are concerned. For whenever the members of a community speak about their landscape—whenever they name it, or classify it, or evaluate it, or move to tell stories about it—they unthinkingly represent it in ways that are compatible with shared understandings of how, in the fullest sense, they know themselves to occupy it. Which is simply to note that in conversational encounters, trivial and otherwise, individuals exchange accounts and observations of the landscape that consistently presuppose (and therefore depend for both their credibility and appropriateness upon) mutually held ideas of what the landscape actually is, why its constituent places are important, and how it may intrude on the practical affairs of its inhabitants. Thus, if frequently by implication and allusion only, bits and pieces of a common world view are given situated relevance and made temporarily accessible. In talk about the landscape, as Martin Heidegger (1977:323) so aptly put it, cultural conceptions of "dwelling together" are naively placed on oblique display.

At the same time, however, and often just as obliquely, persons who engage in this sort of talk will also exchange messages about aspects of the social encounter in which they are jointly involved, including their framings of the encounter itself (i.e., "what is going on here") and their morally guided assessments of the comportment of fellow participants. Consequently, the possibility arises that as speakers communicate about the landscape and the kinds of dealings they have with it, they may also communicate about themselves as social actors and the kinds of dealings they are having with one another. Stated more precisely, statements pertaining to the landscape may be employed to convey indexical messages about the organization of face-to-face relationships and the normative footings on which these relationships are currently being negotiated. Indirectly perhaps, but tellingly all the same, participants in verbal encounters thus put their landscapes to work—interactional work—and how they choose to go about it may shed interesting light on matters other than geography. For example, when a character in a short story by Paul Gallico (1954:69) says to his chronically unfaithful lover, "Go make a nest on Forty-Second Street," it is altogether clear that he is drawing upon the cultural meaning of a place to communicate something important about their disturbed and precarious relationship.

From the standpoint of the ethnographer, then, situated talk of geographical landscapes is more than a valuable resource for exploring local conceptions of the material universe. In addition, and surely just as basic, this sort of talk may be useful for interpreting forms of social action that regularly occur within it, for landscapes are always available to their seasoned inhabitants in other than material terms. Landscapes are available in symbolic terms as well, and so, chiefly through the manifold agencies of speech, they can be "detached" from their fixed spatial moorings and transformed into instruments of thought and vehicles of purposive behavior. Thus transformed, landscapes and the places that fill them become tools for the imagination, expressive means for accomplishing verbal deeds, and also, of course, eminently portable possessions to which individuals can maintain deep and abiding attachments, regardless of where they travel. In these ways, as N. Scott Momaday (1974) has observed, men and women learn to *appropriate* their landscapes, to think and act "with" them as well as about and upon them, and to weave them with spoken words into the very foundations of social life.[1] And in these ways, too, as every ethnographer eventually comes to appreciate, geographical landscapes are never culturally vacant. Filled to brimming with past and present significance, the trick is to try to fathom (and here, really, is where the ethnographic challenge lies) what it is that a particular landscape may be called upon to "say," and what, through the saying, it may be called upon to "do."

But where to begin and how to proceed? How, in any community, to identify the conceptual frameworks and verbal practices with which members appropriate their local geography? One promising approach, I want to suggest, is to attend to native placenames and the full variety of communicative functions served by acts of naming in different social contexts. It may be noted in this regard that placenames, or toponyms, comprise a distinct semantic domain in the lexicons of all known languages, and that the formal properties of placename systems, together with their spatial correlates and etymological histories, have long been objects of anthropological inquiry. But the common activity of placenaming—the actual use of toponyms in concrete instances of everyday speech—has attracted little attention from linguists or ethnographers. Less often still has placenaming been investigated as a universal means—and, it could well turn out, a universally primary means—for appropriating physical environments.

The reasons for this innocuous piece of scholarly neglect are undoubtedly several, but the main one arises from a widespread view of language in which proper names are assumed to have meaning solely in their capacity to refer and, as agents of reference, to enter into simple and complex predications. Many of the limitations imposed by this narrow conception of meaning have been exposed and criticized in recent years, most ably by linguistic anthropologists and philosophers of language who have shown that reference, though unquestionably a vital linguistic function, is but one of many that spoken utterances can be made to perform. But despite these salutary developments, and unhappily for students who seek to understand linguistic meaning as an emergent property of verbal interaction, the idea persists in many quarters that proper names, including top-onyms, serve as referential vehicles whose only purpose is to denote, or "pick out," objects in the world.[2]

If a certain myopia attaches to this position, there is irony as well, for placenames are arguably among the most highly charged and richly evocative of all linguistic symbols. Because of their inseparable connection to specific localities, place-names may be used to summon forth an enormous range of mental and emotional associations—associations of time and space, of history and events, of persons and social activities, of oneself and stages in one's life. And in their capacity to evoke, in their compact power to muster and consolidate so much of what a landscape may be taken to represent in both personal and cultural terms, placenames acquire a functional value that easily matches their utility as instruments of reference. Most notably, as T. S. Eliot (1932) and Seamus Heany (1980) have re-marked, placenames provide materials for resonating ellipses, for speaking and writing in potent shorthand, for communicat-ing much while saying very little. Poets and songwriters have long understood that economy of expression may enhance the quality and force of aesthetic discourse, and that placenames stand ready to be exploited for this purpose. Linguists and an-thropologists would do well to understand that in many com-munities similar considerations may influence common forms of spoken interaction, and that, in this arena too, placenames may occupy a privileged position. For these and other rea-sons, an ethnographic approach to the activity of placenaming seems well worth pursuing. The present essay, which now takes a sharp ethnographic turn, is offered as an illustration of where such an approach may lead, and why, beyond the illumination of specific cases, it may also shed light on matters of general interest.

'Speaking with Names'

The Western Apache residents of Cibecue are not adverse to talking about each other, and some of them—like Lola Machuse—seem to enjoy it immensely. "I'm intress in evy-body!" Lola will exclaim in her distinctive variety of English, and everyone in Cibecue knows she speaks the truth. Just over fifty years old, she is a handsome woman with large brown eyes, a sharply defined nose, and splendidly shaped hands that are hardly ever still. The mother of eight children, she divides her time between caring for the needs of her family, collecting plants for use in herbal medicines, participating in ritual activities, and . . . well, gossiping. Within certain limits, this is just as it should be. Middle-aged Apache women are expected to keep themselves informed at all times of what is going on in their communities, and those who have led exemplary lives, such as Lola Machuse, are also expected to comment on their findings. And comment Lola does—intelligently, incisively, usually sympathetically, and always with an unquenchable enthusiasm for nuance and detail that can be as amusing as it is sometimes overwhelming. Western Apache communities, like small communities everywhere, operate largely by word of mouth, and people from Cibecue have suggested more than once that Lola Machuse is practically a community unto herself.

It is a hot afternoon in the middle of July and Lola Machuse is working at home. Seated in the shade of a large brush-covered ramada, she is mending clothes in the company of her husband, Robert, two Apache women named Emily and Louise, and another visitor, myself, who has come to settle a small debt and get a drink of water.[3] The heat of the afternoon is heavy and oppressive, and there is little to do but gaze at the landscape that stretches out before us: a narrow valley, bisected by a shallow stream lined with cottonwood trees, which rises abruptly to embrace a broken series of red sandstone bluffs, and, beyond the bluffs, a flat expanse of grassy plain ending in the distance at the base of a low range of mountains. Fearsome in the blazing sun, the country around Cibecue lies motionless and inert, thinly shrouded in patches of light bluish haze. Nothing stirs except for Clifford, the Machuses' ancient yellow dog, who shifts his position in the dust, groans fitfully, and snaps at the passing of a fly. Silence.

The silence is broken by Louise, who reaches into her oversized purse for a can of Pepsi-Cola, jerks it open with a loud snap, and begins to speak in the Cibecue dialect of Western Apache. She speaks softly, haltingly, and with long pauses to accentuate the seriousness of what she is saying. Late last night, she reports, sickness assailed her younger brother. Painful cramps gnawed at his stomach. Numbness crept up his legs and into his thighs. He vomited three times in rapid succession. He looked extremely pale. In the morning, just before dawn, he was driven to the hospital at Whiteriver. The people who had gathered at his camp were worried and frightened and talked about what happened. One of them, Louise's cousin, recalled that several months ago, when her brother was working on a cattle roundup near a place named *tsi biyi'itin* ('trail extends into a grove of sticklike trees'), he had inadvertently stepped on a snakeskin that lay wedged in a crevice between some rocks. Another member of the roundup crew, who witnessed the incident, cautioned the young man that contact with snakes is always dangerous and urged him to immediately seek the services of a 'snake medicine person' (*tł'iish diiyin*). But Louise's younger brother had only smiled, remarking tersely that he was not alarmed and that no harm would befall him.

Louise, who is plainly worried and upset by these events, pauses and sips from her drink. After a minute or so, having regained her composure, she begins to speak again. But Lola Machuse quietly interrupts her. Emily and Robert will speak as well. What follows is a record of their discourse, together with English translations of the utterances.[4]

LOUISE: *shidzhé . . .* ("My younger brother . . .")

LOLA: *tsé hadigaiyé yú 'ágodzaa.* ("It happened at line of white rocks extends upward and out, at this very place!")
[Pause: 30–45 seconds]

EMILY: *ha'aa. túzhi' yahigaiyé yú 'ágodzaa.* ("Yes. It happened at whiteness spreads out descending to water, at this very place!")
[Pause: 30–45 seconds]

LOLA: *da'aníí. k'is deeschii' naaditiné yú 'ágodzaa.* ("Truly. It happened at trail extends across a long red ridge with alder trees, at this very place!")

LOUISE: [laughs softly]

ROBERT: *gozhǫǫ dooleeł.* ("Pleasantness and goodness will be forthcoming.")

LOLA: *gozhǫǫ dooleeł.* ("Pleasantness and goodness will be forthcoming.")

LOUISE: *shidizhé bíni'éshid ne góshé!* ("My younger brother is foolish, isn't he, dog?")

Following this brief exchange, talk ceases under the brush-covered ramada and everyone retreats into the privacy of their own thoughts. Louise drinks again from her can of Pepsi-Cola and passes it on to Emily. Lola Machuse returns to her sewing, while Robert studies a horse in a nearby corral. Only Clifford, who has launched a feverish attack on an itch below his ear, seems unaffected by what has been said. Silence once again.

But what *has* been said? To what set of personal and social ends? And why in such a clipped and cryptic fashion? If these questions create problems for us (and that they do, I think, can be assumed), it is because we are dealing with a spate of conversation whose organization eludes us, a strip of Western Apache verbal doings whose animating aims and purposes seem obscure. But why? The problem is not that the literal meanings of utterances comprising the conversation are in any way difficult to grasp. On the contrary, anyone with a passing knowledge of Western Apache grammar could attest that each of the utterances, taken as a sentence type, is well-formed in all respects, and that each presents one or more simple claims whose positive truth-value no Apache would presume to dispute. It is not, then, on the surface of the utterances—or, as some linguists might prefer to say, at the level of their propositional content—where our interpretive difficulties lie.

What is puzzling about this snippet of Western Apache talk is that we are unable to account for the ways in which its constituent utterances are related to each other. Put more exactly, we lack the knowledge required to establish sequential relations among the utterances, the unstated premises and assumptions that order the utterances, just as they occur, into a piece of meaningful discourse. It is by no means evident, for example, how Lola Machuse's statement ("It happened at line of white rocks extends upward and out, at this very place!") should be related to Louise's narrative about her ailing brother. Neither is it clear how Emily's assertion ("Yes. It happened at whiteness spreads out descending to water, at this very place!") should be interpreted as a response to the narrative or to Lola's statement. What are we to make of Lola's response to Emily ("Truly. It happened at trail extends across a long red ridge with alder trees, at this very place!"); and why should it be, as things are coming to a close, that Louise sees fit to address the Machuses' dog? Our puzzlement persists throughout, causing us to experience the text of the conversation as fragmented and disjointed, as oddly unmotivated, as failing to come together as a whole. In short, we are unable to place a construction on the text that invests it with *coherence,* and so, in the end, we cannot know with any certainty what the conversation itself may have been about. Lola Machuse and her companions have surely accomplished something with their talk. But what?

The episode at Cibecue exemplifies a venerable practice with which Western Apache speakers exploit the evocative power of placenames to comment on the moral conduct of persons who are absent from the scene. Called 'speaking with names' (*yałti'bee'ízhi*), this verbal routine also allows those who engage in it to register claims about their own moral worth, aspects of their social relationships with other people on hand, and a particular way of attending to the local landscape that is avowed to produce a beneficial form of heightened self-awareness. And as if this were not enough, much of what gets said and done is attributed to unseen 'ancestors' (*nohwizą'yé*) who are prompted by the voices of conversational participants to communicate in a collective voice that no one actually hears. All in all, as one can see, 'speaking with names' is a rather subtle and subterranean affair.

To reach an understanding of this practice and the sources of its coherence for Western Apache people, I shall assume that spoken discourse is a cooperative activity in which individuals seek, within the bounds of negotiated social proprieties, to accomplish a range of communicative purposes. I shall also assume that participants in many kinds of discourse use language to explore with each other the significance of past and potential events, drawing from these examinations certain consequences for their present and future actions. Finally, I shall assume that speakers pursue such objectives by producing utterances that are intended to perform several speech acts simultaneously, and that hearers, making dexterous use of relevant bodies of cultural knowledge, react and respond to them at different levels of abstraction. Spoken discourse, then, is more than a chain of situated utterances. Rather, as William Labov and David Fanshel (1977:26–28) have shown, discourse consists in a developing matrix of utterances and actions, bound together by a web of shared understandings pertinent to both, which serves as an expanding context for interpreting the meanings of utterances and actions alike. More a matter of linguistic function than linguistic form, coherence in discourse is achieved when participants put their utterances to interlocking forms of mutually recognizable work. More a matter of implicit doings than explicit sayings, coherence is what participants hear (though generally they fail to notice hearing it) when their work is going well.

At Lola Machuse's somnolent camp, where the work of discourse went off without a hitch, coherence was never in question. Neither was the smooth implementation of a Western Apache technique for appropriating the natural landscape, a distinctive cultural framework for interpreting the landscape and turning it by means of speech to specific social ends. Never in question, that is, to anyone but myself—a superfluous, slightly stupefied, and keenly perplexed outsider. What the devil did Lola Machuse and those other Apaches imagine themselves to be up to as they sat around swapping placenames? How were they making sense, and what sort of sense were they making? What manner of thinking informed their utterances and the actions their utterances performed? What, in short, was the culture of their discourse?

"We Gave That Woman Pictures . . ."

If the discourse at Lola Machuse's camp is to be usefully understood, if we are to grasp its coherence and appreciate the
structure of its interactional design, steps must be taken to enter the conceptual world of the Western Apache people who
produced it. Needless to say, we cannot recover their experience
of their discourse as it actually occurred, what the phenome-
nologist Merleau-Ponty (1969:89) called the "inner experience
of language-spoken-now." But we can explore, perforce retro-
spectively and therefore in reconstructive terms, what participants in the encounter took their discourse to be about, why
they saw fit to contribute to it as they did, and how they interpreted the utterances and actions that comprised it. In addition,
and certainly just as important, we can explore the culturally
based assumptions and beliefs that made these interpretations
possible, the "linguistic ideology" with which people from
Cibecue rationalize for themselves and explain to others what
spoken words are capable of doing when used in certain ways.[5]
In short, we can construct an ethnographic account of the
speech event itself, an interpretation of Apache interpretations
that relates the event to the body of thought that made its occurrence meaningful and to the particular social circumstances
that made its meaning unique.

All such undertakings profit from the guidance of experienced native instructors, and no one living at Cibecue is more
capable or willing in this regard than Lola Machuse herself. So
let us begin, as in fact I did shortly after the episode at her camp
took place, by considering her account of what transpired as the
women drank their Pepsi and Clifford snapped at flies.

> We gave that woman [i.e., Louise] pictures to work on in her
> mind. We didn't speak too much to her. We didn't hold her
> down. That way she could travel in her mind. She could add on
> to them [i.e., the pictures] easily. We gave her clear pictures
> with placenames. So her mind went to those places, standing in
> front of them as our ancestors did long ago. That way she could
> see what happened there long ago. She could hear stories in her
> mind, perhaps hear our ancestors speaking. She could reknow

the wisdom of our ancestors. We call it speaking with names. Placenames are all we need for that, speaking with names. We just fix them up. That woman was too sad. She was worried too much about her younger brother. So we tried to make her feel better. We tried to make her think good thoughts. That woman's younger brother acted stupidly. He was stupid and careless. He failed to show respect. No good! We said nothing critical about him to her. We talked around it. Those placenames are strong! After a while, I gave her a funny story. She didn't get mad. She was feeling better. She laughed. Then she had enough, I guess. She spoke to the dog about her younger brother, criticizing him, so we knew we had helped her out.

Lola Machuse recorded this statement two days after the speech event at her camp took place, and four days later, having discussed her account with all parties involved, I determined to treat it as a guide for subsequent research. Everyone to whom I presented Lola's account agreed that it was encompassing and astute; it touched, they said, on everything that was essential for getting a proper sense of what 'speaking with names' might be used to accomplish. But they also agreed that it was rather too highly condensed, a bare bones sort of interpretation (certainly adequate for persons already familiar with the practice, but understandably opaque to a neophyte such as myself) which could profit from explication and fleshing out. Never one to be outdone, Lola Machuse agreed instantly with the agreers, saying she was well aware of the problem, thank you very much, and had understood all along that further instruction would be necessary. Sometimes talk is complicated, she admonished, and one must move slowly to get to the bottom of it. So with all of us scrambling to agree with Lola, and with Lola herself firmly in charge, the fleshing out process began. Our work took longer than I expected, but now, with much of it done, Lola Machuse's original account seems better to me than ever; it provides, as one of my older Apache consultants told me it would, a "straight path to knowing." And so I have used Lola's interpretation here, partitioned into convenient segments, as a model, a path of a different kind, for organizing and presenting my own.

We gave that woman pictures to work on in her mind. We didn't speak too much to her. We didn't hold her down. That way she could travel in her mind. She could add on to them easily.

Western Apache conceptions of language and thought are cast in pervasively visual terms. Every occasion of 'speaking' (*yałti'*) provides tangible evidence of 'thinking' (*natsíkees*), and thinking, which Apaches describe as an intermittent and variably intense activity, occurs in the form of 'pictures' (*be'elzaahí*) that persons 'see' (*yo'įį*) in their 'minds' (*biini'*). Prompted by a desire to 'display thinking' (*nil'íí natsíkees*), speaking involves the use of language to 'depict' (*'e'ele'*) and 'carry' (*yo'ááł*) these mental images to the members of an audience, such that they, on 'hearing' (*yidits'ag*) and 'holding' (*yotą́'*) the speaker's words, can 'view' (*yínel'įį'*) facsimiles of his or her images in their own minds. Thinking, as the Apache conceive of it, consists in picturing to oneself and attending privately to the pictures. Speaking consists in depicting one's pictures for other people, who are thus invited to picture these depictions and respond to them with depictions of pictures of their own. Discourse, or 'conversation' (*'iłch'į' yádaach'ilti'*), consists in a running exchange of depicted pictures and pictured depictions, a reciprocal representation and visualization of the ongoing thoughts of participating speakers.

But things are not really so neat and tidy. According to consultants from Cibecue, the depictions offered by Western Apache speakers are invariably incomplete. Even the most gifted and proficient speakers contrive to leave things out, and small children, who have not yet learned to indulge in such contrivances, leave out many things. Consequently, Apache hearers must always 'add on' (*'inágoda'aah*) to depictions made available to them in conversation, augmenting and supplementing these spoken images with images they fashion for themselves. This process—the picturing, or viewing, of other people's verbal depictions—is commonly likened to adding stones to a partially finished wall (or laying bricks upon the foundation of a house) because it is understood to involve a 'piling up' (*łik'iyitł'ih*) of new materials onto like materials already in place. It is also said to resemble the rounding up of livestock: the 'bringing together' (*dalaházhį'ch'indííł*) of cattle or horses from widely scattered locations to a central place where other animals have been previously gathered. These metaphors all point to the same general idea, which is that depictions provided by Apache speakers are treated by Apache hearers as bases on which to build, as projects to complete, as invitations to exercise the imagination.

The Western Apache regard spoken conversation as a form of 'voluntary cooperation' (*łich'į' 'odaach'idii*) in which all participants, having presumably come together in the spirit of good will, are entitled to displays of 'respect' (*yińłsįh*). Accordingly, whenever people speak in cordial and affable tones, considerations of 'kindness and politeness' (*bił goch'oba'*) come centrally into play. Such considerations may influence Apache speech in a multitude of ways, but none is more basic than the courtesy speakers display by refraining from 'speaking too much' (*łąągo yałti'*). Although the effects of this injunction are most clearly evident in the spare verbal style employed by experienced Apache storytellers, people from Cibecue insist that all forms of narration stand to benefit from its application. And the reasons, they explain, are simple enough.

A person who speaks too much—someone who describes too busily, who supplies too many details, who repeats and qualifies too many times—presumes without warrant on the right of hearers to build freely and creatively on the speaker's own depictions. With too many words, such a speaker acts to 'smother' (*biká' nyinłkaad*) his or her audience by seeming to say, arrogantly and coercively, "I *demand* that you see everything that happened, how it happened, and why it happened, *exactly* as I do." In other words, persons who speak too much insult the imaginative capabilities of other people, "blocking their thinking," as one of my consultants put it in English, and "holding down their minds." So Western Apache narrators consistently take a very different tack, implying by the economical manner of their speech, "I will depict just enough for you to see what happened, how it happened, and perhaps why it happened. Add on to these depictions however you see fit." An effective narrator, people from Cibecue report, never speaks too much. An effective narrator, they say, takes steps to "open up thinking," thereby encouraging his or her listeners to "travel in their minds."[6]

> We gave her clear pictures with placenames. So her mind went to those places, standing in front of them as our ancestors did long ago. That way she could see what happened there long ago. She could hear stories in her mind, perhaps hear our ancestors speaking. She could reknow the wisdom of our ancestors.

Nothing is considered more basic to the effective telling of a Western Apache 'story' or 'narrative' (nagoldi'é) than identifying the geographical locations at which events in the story unfold. For unless Apache listeners are able to picture a physical setting for narrated events (unless, as one of my consultants said, "your mind can travel to the place and really see it"), the events themselves will be difficult to imagine. This is because events in the narrative will seem to 'happen nowhere' (doohwaa 'ágodzaa da), and such an idea, Apaches assert, is both preposterous and disquieting. Placeless events are an impossibility; everything that happens must happen somewhere. The location of an event is an integral aspect of the event itself, and therefore identifying the event's location is essential to properly depicting—and effectively picturing—the event's occurrence. For these reasons, people from Cibecue explain, placeless stories simply do not get told. Instead, to borrow a useful phrase from the linguist Harry Hoijer (personal communication, 1973), all Western Apache narratives are "spatially anchored" to points upon the land with precise depictions of specific locations. And what these depictions are accomplished with—what the primary spatial anchors of Apache narratives almost always turn out to be—are 'placenames' (ni'bízhi'; literally, 'land names').

The great majority of Western Apache placenames currently in use are believed to have been created long ago by the 'ancestors' (nohwizá'yé) of the Apache people. The ancestors, who had to travel constantly in search of food, covered vast amounts of territory and needed to be able to remember and discuss many different locations. This was facilitated by the invention of hundreds of descriptive placenames that were intended to depict their referents in close and exact detail. In this important undertaking, as in many others, the ancestors were eminently successful. Today, as undoubtedly for centuries before, Apaches observe with evident satisfaction that the mental pictures evoked by placenames are 'accurate' (da'áíyee) and 'correct' (dábik'eh). Again and again, people from Cibecue report, ancestral placenames bring graphically to mind the locations they depict.[7]

Some appreciation of the descriptive precision of Western Apache placenames can be gained by matching names with photographs of their referents. By way of illustration, consider the three names listed below, which have been segmented into their gross morphological constituents and whose referents are shown in figures 16–18.

1. t'iis bitł'áh tú 'olįį́': t'iis ('cottonwood tree') + bitł'áh ('below it', 'underneath it') + tú ('water') + o- ('inward') + lįį́' ('it flows').

Gloss: 'water flows inward underneath a cottonwood tree'

2. tséłigaí dah sidil: tsé ('rock', 'stone') + łigaí ('white') + dah ('above ground level') + sidil ('three or more form a compact cluster').

Gloss: 'white rocks lie above in a compact cluster'

3. tsé biká' tú yahilįį́': tsé ('rock', 'stone') + biká' ('on top of it'; a flattish object) + tú ('water') + ya- ('downward') + -hi- ('linear succession of regularly repeated movements') + -lįį́' ('it flows').

Gloss: 'water flows down on top of a regular succession of flat rocks'

As shown by the photographs, Western Apache placenames provide more than precise depictions of the sites to which the names may be used to refer. In addition, placenames implicitly identify positions for viewing these locations: optimal vantage points, so to speak, from which the sites can be observed, clearly and unmistakably, just as their names depict them. To picture a site from its name, then, requires that one imagine it as if standing or sitting at a particular spot, and it is to these

FIGURE 16. *t'iis bitł'áh tú 'olíí'* ('water flows inward underneath a cottonwood tree').

privileged positions, Apaches say, that the images evoked by placenames cause them to travel in their minds.

Wherever the optimal vantage point for a named site may be located—east of the site or west, above it or below, near it or at some distance away—the vantage point is described as being 'in front of' (*bádnyú*) the site; and it is here, centuries ago, that ancestors of the Western Apache are believed to have stood when they gave the site its name. Accordingly, consultants from Cibecue explain that in positioning people's minds to look 'forward' (*bidááh*) into space, a placename also positions their minds to look 'backward' (*t'ąązhi'*) into time. For as persons imagine themselves standing in front of a named site, they may imagine that they are standing in their 'ancestors' tracks' (*nohwizą'yé biké'é*), and from this psychological perspective, which is sometimes described as an intense form of 'daydreaming' (*bił*

FIGURE 17. *tsé łigai dah sidil* ('white rocks live above in a compact cluster').

onaagodah), traditional accounts of ancestral events associated with the site are said to be recalled with singular clarity and force. In other words, by evoking detailed pictures of places, together with specific vantage points from which to picture picturing them, placenames acquire a capacity to evoke stories and images of the people who knew the places first. When placenames are used by Apache speakers in certain ways, mental pictures of the ancestors come instantly and vividly alive.

The capacity of Western Apache placenames to situate people's minds in historical time and space is clearly apparent when names are used to anchor traditional narratives—'myths' (*godiyįhgo nagoldi'é*), 'sagas' (*nłt'éégo nagoldi'é*), and 'historical tales' (*'ágodzaahí nagoldi'é*)—which present depictions of 'ancestral life' (*nohwizą'yé zhineego*) and, in so doing, illustrate aspects of 'ancestral wisdom' (*nohwizą'yé bi kigoyą'íí*).[8] But

FIGURE 18. *tsé biká' tú yahilįį'* ('water flows down on top of a regular succession of flat rocks').

the evocative power of placenames is most dramatically displayed when a name is used to substitute for the narrative it anchors, 'standing up alone' (*'o'áá*), as Apaches say, to symbolize the narrative as well as the wisdom it contains. On such occasions, consultants from Cibecue report, a single placename may accomplish the communicative work of an entire saga or historical tale; and sometimes, depending on the immediate social circumstances, it may accomplish even more. For when placenames are employed in this isolated and autonomous fashion—when, in other words, Apache people practice 'speaking with names'—their actions are interpreted as a recommendation to recall ancestral wisdom and apply it directly to matters of pressing personal concern. And in emotionally charged contexts like these, my consultants maintain, 'ancestral voices' (*nohwizą'yé bizhíí*) may seem to speak directly to the individuals involved.[9]

We call it speaking with names. Placenames are all we need for that, speaking with names. We just fix them up. That woman was too sad. She was worried too much about her younger brother. So we tried to make her feel better. We tried to make her think good thoughts.

'Speaking with names' is considered appropriate under certain conditions only, and these conditions, which Apaches describe as socially 'taut' (*ndoh*) and 'heavy' (*ndaaz*), tend to occur infrequently. Consequently, as people from Cibecue are quick to point out, placenames are usually put to other communicative ends. Most of the time, in the recurrent situations supplied by everyday life, placenames are called upon to perform simple verbal chores: to indicate where one is going, for example, or to announce where one has been; to make plans for a forthcoming hunt, or to pinpoint the latest happenings gleaned from local gossip. When placenames are used for ordinary purposes such as these, Apache speakers typically produce the names in shortened or contracted forms. Thus, the name *t'iis bitłah tú olíí'* ('water flows inward underneath a cottonwood tree') is commonly heard as *t'iis tl'áh 'olíí'* or *t'iis tú 'olíí'*, the name *tsé biká' tú yahilíí'* ('water flows down on top of a regular succession of flat rocks') as *tsé ká' yahilíí'* or *tsé tú yahilíí'*, and so forth. In marked contrast to these abbreviated renderings, placenames intended to evoke mental pictures of the past are invariably spoken in full and are embellished, or 'fixed up' (*náyidlé*), with an optional suffix that imparts an emphatic force roughly equivalent to English "right here!" or "at this very place!" Accordingly, the placename *t'iis bitł'áh tú olíí'* is produced in traditional narratives as *t'iis bitł'áh tú' olíné*, the name *tsé biká' tú yahilíí'* as *tsé biká' tú yahilíné*, etc. Although the optional suffix may be employed for purposes other than helping to summon ancestral images and voices, my consultants agree that this is one of its primary functions. And at no time is that function more readily apparent as when Apache men and women, bent upon 'speaking with names', dispense with narratives completely and use placenames, fully encliticized, in the expression *X 'ágodzaa yú* ("It happened at X, at this very place!").

This expression is normally reserved for social situations in which speaking of absent parties to persons closely connected to them must be accomplished with delicacy and tact. More specifically, the expression is used when ancestral wisdom seems applicable to difficulties arising from serious errors in someone else's judgment, but when voicing one's thoughts on the matter—or, as one of my consultants said, "making wisdom too plain"—might be taken as evidence of moral conceit, critical disapproval, and a lack of sympathetic understanding. Instead, and ever so deftly, 'speaking with names' enables those who engage in it to acknowledge a regrettable circumstance without explicitly judging it, to exhibit solicitude without openly proclaiming it, and to offer advice without appearing to do so.

But 'speaking with names' accomplishes more than this. A traditional Apache narrative encapsulated in its own spatial anchor, the expression X 'ágodzaa yú is also a call to memory and imagination. Simultaneously, it is a call to persons burdened by worry and despair to take remedial action on behalf of themselves. "Travel in your mind," the expression urges those to whom it is addressed. "Travel in your mind to a point from which to view the place whose name has just been spoken. Imagine standing there, as if in the tracks of your ancestors, and recall stories of events that occurred at that place long ago. Picture these events in your mind and appreciate, as if the ancestors themselves were speaking, the wisdom the stories contain. Bring this wisdom to bear on your own disturbing situation. Allow the past to inform your understanding of the present. You will feel better if you do."

And Western Apache people report that sometimes they do feel better. Having pictured distant places and dwelled on distant events, their worries may become less plaguing and acute: less 'sharp' (ts'ik'ii), less 'rigid' (ntł'iz), less 'noisy' (gonch'add) in their minds. Feelings of anxiety and emotional turbulence may give way to welcome sensations of 'smoothness' (dilkǫǫh), of 'softness' (dédi'ilé), of growing inner 'quiet' (doohwaa-gonch'aada). And when this actually happens—when ancestral wisdom works to give beneficial perspective and fresh recognition that trying times can be dealt with successfully and eventually overcome—persons thus heartened may announce that relationships characterized by 'pleasantness and goodness' (*goozhǫǫ*) have been restored between themselves and their surroundings. A psychological balance has been reestablished, an optimistic outlook borne of strengthened confidence and rejuvenated hope, and people may also announce that a 'sickness' (*nezgai*) has been 'healed' (*nábilziih*). 'Bad thinking' (*nchǫ'go natsíkęęs*) has been replaced by 'good thinking' (*nzhǫǫgo natsíkęęs*), and at least for a while the exigencies of life can be met with replenished equanimity.

"Those Placenames Are Strong"

The foregoing account of aspects of Western Apache placename ideology supplies the basic conceptual framework with which to interpret the conversational encounter at Lola Machuse's camp in Cibecue. But because the account has been formulated as Apache people themselves insist upon doing—that is, in abstract normative terms—it fails to elucidate what the practice of 'speaking with names' served to accomplish on that particular occasion. In other words, we have yet to identify the social actions that participants in the encounter used their utterances to perform, and thus, necessarily, we have yet to grasp the coherence of their talk. So let us be about it. Having fashioned an account of the cultural logic on which 'speaking with names' is understood to operate, attention may now be directed to a functional interpretation of how, and with what sorts of interpersonal consequences, this mode of discourse was actually put to work. Once again, Lola Machuse.

> That woman's younger brother acted stupidly. He was stupid and careless. He failed to show respect. No good! We said nothing critical about him to her. We talked around it.

The social gathering at Lola Machuse's camp was uncomfortable for everyone involved, but especially for Louise. Troubled by her brother's sudden illness, she was troubled even more by his apparent lack of common sense. Having come into contact with the snakeskin near the roundup camp, he should have gone directly to a ritual specialist for assistance in dealing with his contaminated state. That he failed to do so was disturbing enough, but that he treated the incident in such a cavalier fashion was more disturbing still. Plainly, he was guilty of a grave lapse in judgment, and now, as surely he could have anticipated, he was suffering the painful consequences. Why had the young man acted so irresponsibly? In addition to being upset, Louise was bewildered and perplexed.

Louise's chronicle of her brother's misfortune created an opportunity for all on hand to comment on his conduct. But because her account portrayed him in a distinctly unfavorable light, it also presented him as a target for easy criticism. If criticism were to be forthcoming, it could only serve to embarrass Louise, for she would have no alternative but to try to defend her brother's actions—and this would be awkward and difficult at best. Yet refusing to defend him could be taken to mean that she was prepared to condemn him entirely, and condemning one's relatives, especially in the presence of nonrelatives, is a conspicuous violation of kinship loyalties that Western Apaches rarely see fit to excuse.[10]

For these reasons, Louise's candid statement placed her companions in a delicate dilemma. On the one hand, no one could assert that Louise's brother had not acted wrongly without casting serious doubt on his or her own good judgment. On the other hand, no one could openly censure the young man without adding to Louise's discomfort, thereby displaying a lack of considerateness for her aggravated feelings and a lack of concern for the circumstances that had produced them. How, then, to respond? How to speak the truth—or something that could be heard as not denying the truth—without exacerbating an already sensitive situation?

> Those placenames really helped us out! We gave her pictures with placenames. That way she started feeling better. Those placenames are strong!

After finishing her account, Louise paused, took a long drink from her Pepsi-Cola, and started to speak again of her beleaguered brother. But Lola Machuse intervened at this point, saying softly but firmly, "*tsé hadigaiyé yú 'ágodzaa'* " ("It happened at line of white rocks extends upward and out, at this very place!"). Lola's utterance was intended to evoke a historical tale for Louise to picture in her mind, but it was also designed to change the topic of talk and set the conversation on a new and different course. Instead of Louise's brother, whom Lola was showing she had no desire to criticize, attention was shifted to Louise herself and her troubled reactions to her brother's unfortunate predicament. Instead of disapproval, Lola Machuse was exhibiting sympathy and concern.

As later told by herself, the historical tale that Lola Machuse wished to evoke is the following.

It happened at line of white rocks extends upward and out.
Long ago, a girl lived alone with her maternal grandmother. Her grandmother sent her out regularly to collect firewood. She went to a place above her camp. She could get there quickly by climbing up through a rocky canyon. Many snakes lived there. So her grandmother told her always to go another way.
The girl went to collect firewood. The day was hot. Then the girl became thirsty. Then she thought, "This wood is heavy. I don't want to carry it too far." Then she started to walk down the rocky canyon. There were loose rocks where she walked. Then she slipped and fell down. The firewood she was carrying scattered everywhere! Then she started to pick it up. A snake bit her hand! Then she got scared. "My grandmother knew this would happen to me," she thought.
Then the girl returned to where she was living with her grandmother. Her arm and hand became badly swollen. Then they worked over her [i.e., performed a curing ceremony]. Later, the girl went to her grandmother. "My life is still my own," she said. Then her grandmother talked to her again. Now she knew how to live right.
It happened at line of white rocks extends upward and out.

As Lola Machuse had reason to suspect, Louise knew this story well. She had heard it many times and on several occasions had performed it for her own children. Consequently, Louise reported later, her mind traveled instantly to a spot from which to view the place named *tsé hadigai* ('line of white rocks extends upward and out'), and images of the girl carrying firewood—and, most vividly of all, of the girl's scrambling attempts to retrieve it after she lost her footing—appeared just as quickly. As a lengthy silence descended on the Machuse camp at Cibecue, Louise's thoughts moved along these lines.

> A bad thing happened at that place. Very bad! I saw that girl. She was impulsive. She forgot to be careful. She ceased showing respect. She was like my younger brother. She ceased thinking properly, so something bad happened to her. She became very scared but recovered from it. She almost died but held onto her own life.

Lola Machuse's evocative comment had a calming effect on everyone sitting beneath the ramada at her home. Her statement relieved Louise of any need to publicly defend her brother's conduct and, at the same time, charted a conversational path that others could easily follow. Acknowledging the felicity of that path, and taking steps to pursue it, Emily produced a similar statement of her own—*"ha'aa. túzhí yahigaiyé yú 'ágodzaa."* ("Yes. It happened at whiteness spreads out descending to water, at this very place!")—and once again Louise was urged to travel in her mind and picture a historical tale.

Emily's version of this tale, which she said has been slightly abridged, is as follows.

> It happened at whiteness spreads out descending to water.
> Long ago, a boy went to hunt deer. He rode on horseback. Pretty soon he saw one [a deer], standing on the side of a canyon. Then he went closer and shot it. He killed it. Then the deer rolled all the way down to the bottom of the canyon.
> Then the boy went down there. It was a buck, fat and muscular. Then he butchered it. The meat was heavy, so he had to carry it up in pieces. He had a hard time reaching the top of the canyon with each piece.
> Now it was getting dark. One hindquarter was still laying at the bottom of the canyon. "I have enough meat already," he thought. So he left the hindquarter where it was lying. He left it there.
> Then he packed his horse and started to ride home. Then the boy got dizzy and nearly fell off his horse. Then his nose

twitched uncontrollably, like Deer's nose does. Then pain shot
up behind his eyes. Then he became scared.

Now he went back to the canyon. It was dark when he got
there. He walked down to where the hindquarter was lying—
but it was gone! Then he returned to his horse. He rode fast to
where he was living with his relatives.

The boy was sick for a long time. The people prayed for him
on four separate occasions. He got better slowly.

Some time after that, when the boy had grown to manhood,
he always had bad luck in hunting. No deer would present
themselves to him. He said to his children: "Look at me now. I
failed to be careful when I was a boy and now I have a hard time
getting meat for you to eat."

It happened at whiteness spreads out descending to water.

The actions performed by Emily's utterance were readily apparent to Louise. Emily, like Lola Machuse before her, was attempting to distract Louise with constructive thoughts and
comfort her with expressions of support. But Louise was not
intimately familiar with the story of the boy and the deer, and
though her mind went swiftly to a point near *túzhį' yahigai*
('whiteness spreads out descending to water'), she had difficulty
picturing all the events in the story. She did, however, have one
vivid image—of the pain-ridden boy struggling to stay astride
his horse—and this was sufficient to remind her of her brother.
In addition, Louise said later, she could hear the boy, now an
adult, as he spoke to his children about his fateful mistake.

It was like I could hear some old man talking. He was talking to
his children. "I was impatient, so I left behind good meat from
that deer. Then I became very sick and very scared. I failed to
show respect." Even so, that boy lived on and grew up and had
children. He learned to think right, so he talked to his children
about it. Maybe my brother will learn to improve his thinking
like that.

The historical tale evoked by Emily is similar in several respects to the tale evoked by Lola Machuse, and at this point in
the proceedings, Louise probably sensed that a definite pattern
was starting to form. In both of the stories, young people are

depicted as irresponsible and disrespectful, but for reasons having solely to do with their innocence and naivete. In both stories, they suffer life-threatening consequences—serious illness and intense fright—from which they learn to avoid carelessness and impatience in the future. Finally, and most important of all, they regain their health and continue living, presumably for many years. Thus the unstated message for Louise, which is also a prominent aspect of Western Apache ancestral wisdom, was a distinctly positive one: in effect, "Take heart. These things will happen. Young people make foolish and dangerous mistakes, but they usually profit from them and the mistakes are seldom fatal. Be optimistic. There is reason to believe your brother will recover."

> After a while, I gave her a funny story. She didn't get mad. She was feeling better. She laughed. Then she had enough, I guess. She spoke to the dog about her younger brother, criticizing him, so we knew we had helped her out.

Following another lengthy silence inside the brush-covered ramada, Lola Machuse acted to affirm and consolidate the tacit messages communicated thus far with a placename intended to evoke a third historical tale with similarities to the previous two. But with this utterance—*"da'aníí. k'is deeschii' naaditiné yú 'ágodzaa."* ("Truly. It happened at trail extends across a long red ridge with alder trees, at this very place!")—Lola took a moderate social risk. Although it deals with serious matters, the story Lola was thinking of presents a humorous aspect, and one of her purposes in evoking it was to lighten Louise's spirits (and everyone else's) by striking a note of reserved good cheer. The risk Lola ran was that her action would be perceived as intemperate, perhaps even playful, and thus inappropriate to the solemnity of Louise's circumstances.

This is the historical tale, as narrated by herself, that Lola Machuse had in mind.

> It happened at trail extends across a long red ridge with alder trees.
> A boy and a girl were newly married. He didn't know that he

should stay away from her when her grandmother came to visit [i.e., when she was having her menstrual period]. Then he tried to bother her. "Don't! I'm no good for that," she said. He was impatient. Then he tried to bother her again. Then she gave in.

Then the boy got sick, they say. It was hard for him to sit down. Then his penis became badly swollen. Pissing was painful for him, too. He walked around clutching his crotch. He was deeply embarrassed in front of his wife and her relatives. Then he got scared. "I wonder if I will be this way forever," he thought.

Then someone talked to him, saying "Don't bother your wife when her grandmother comes to visit. Stay away from her." Then that person gave the boy some medicine, saying "Drink this. It will make you well. Then you can stop being embarrassed. Then you can stop walking around clutching your crotch!" That is all.

It happened at trail extends across a long red ridge with alder trees.

Fortunately, Lola Machuse's lighthearted gamble did not misfire. Louise's mind traveled to a vantage point from which to picture *k'is deeschii' naaditiné* ('trail extends across a long red ridge with alder trees'), viewed the crestfallen lad with his hand where it should never be seen in public, and returned from the journey with Louise mildly amused. Afterwards, Louise made these comments.

Everyone knows that story. My mind went there. It's funny to see that boy in the story holding onto himself. He should have left his wife alone. He was impulsive. He didn't think right. Then he got scared. Then he was made well again with medicine. . . . I've heard that story often, but it's always funny to see that boy holding onto himself, so shy and embarrassed.

At the Machuse camp in Cibecue, Louise expressed her amusement by laughing softly. This was an auspicious sign! Though sorely worried still, Louise had been moved to levity and everyone could tell that her spirits had briefly improved. Here was evidence that the unspoken messages conveyed by Lola Machuse and Emily—messages of sympathy, consolation, and encouragement—had been beneficially received. Here was an indication that ancestral wisdom was providing Louise with a measure of comfort and hope. Seizing the moment, Robert Machuse acted to make elements of these messages explicit, compressing their dominant thrust into one succinct statement. *"gozhǫǫ doleeł"* ("Pleasantness and goodness will be forthcoming"), said Robert with quiet conviction. And moments later, endorsing his sentiments and adding conviction of her own, Lola Machuse repeated the same phrase: *"gozhǫǫ doleeł"* ("Pleasantness and goodness will be forthcoming").

Touched by this friendly display of goodwill, and well aware that some sort of acknowledgment of it would soon be in order, Louise responded by taking a deft and self-effacing step. In the form of a mock question addressed to Clifford, the Machuses' dog, she gently criticized her own brother: *"shidizhé bíni'éshid ne góshé?"* ("My younger brother is foolish, isn't he, dog?"). This utterance accomplished several actions simultaneously. First, by drawing attention away from herself, Louise gave notice that further evocations of traditional narratives could be politely dispensed with; in effect, "You have all done enough." Also, by directing her question to one who could not answer it, Louise indicated that additional discussion of her brother and his difficulties would serve no useful purpose; in effect, "Let the matter rest. There is nothing more to say." Finally, and most adroitly of all, by voicing the thought that had been on everyone's mind from the beginning—that Louise's brother had indeed acted foolishly—she contrived to thank them for their tact in not having voiced it; in effect, "This is the discrediting truth about my relative. I know it and I know that you know it. You were polite and thoughtful to refrain from expressing it."

As could have been predicted, Clifford did not respond to Louise's bogus query. Neither did anyone else. The speech event was over. A few minutes later, Louise and Emily rose to their feet, complained to each other about a sudden plentitude of flies, and set off together in search of a cold can of Pepsi-Cola. Lola Machuse resumed her sewing and Robert Machuse went to water his horse. The day was beginning to cool, and the landscape beyond Cibecue, its rugged contours softened now by patches of lengthening shadow, looked somewhat more hospitable than before.

Language, Landscape, and the Moral Imagination

The possibilities of human language are variously conceived and variously understood. Every culture, whether literate or not, includes beliefs about how language works and what it is capable of accomplishing. Similarly, every culture contains beliefs about the kinds of social contexts in which these capabilities may be realized most effectively. That such beliefs are present in contemporary Western Apache culture should now be obvious, and that they may operate in direct and telling ways to influence patterns of verbal interaction should likewise be apparent. Moreover, it should now be possible to appreciate how aspects of Western Apache linguistic ideology contribute to perceptions of coherence in one form of Apache discourse, and also why, when contextual conditions are right, that same ideology may invest the briefest of utterances with ample meaning and substantial expressive force.

The episode at Lola Machuse's camp suggests that while coherence in Western Apache discourse can be usefully described as a product of interlocking utterances and actions, the expressive force of Apache discourse—what people from Cibecue call its 'strength' (nalwod)—may be viewed as a product of multiple interlockings at different levels of abstraction. Put more exactly, it is my impression that those utterances that perform the broadest range of mutually compatible actions at once are those that Apaches experience as having the greatest communicative impact. In other words, the expressive force of an Apache utterance seems to be roughly proportionate to the number of separate but complementary functions it accomplishes simultaneously, or, as Alton Becker (1982) has intimated, to the number of distinguishable subject matters it successfully communicates about.

The Western Apache practice of 'speaking with names' manifests just this sort of functional range and versatility. Thus, as we have seen, an utterance such as *tsé hadigaiyé yú 'ágodzaa* ('It happened at line of white rocks extends upward and out, at this very place!') may be understood to accomplish all of the following actions: (1) produce a mental image of a particular geographical location; (2) evoke prior texts, such as historical tales and sagas; (3) affirm the value and validity of traditional moral precepts (i.e., ancestral wisdom); (4) display tactful and courteous attention to aspects of both positive and negative face; (5) convey sentiments of charitable concern and personal support; (6) offer practical advice for dealing with disturbing personal circumstances (i.e., apply ancestral wisdom); (7) transform distressing thoughts caused by excessive worry into more agreeable ones marked by optimism and hopefulness; (8) heal wounded spirits.

This is a substantial amount for any spoken utterance to be capable of accomplishing, and what provides for the capability—what the forceful activity of 'speaking with names' always communicates most basically "about"—is the cultural importance of named locations within the Western Apache landscape. Named places have long been symbols of mythic significance for the Apache people, and placenames—symbols that designate these symbols—supply Apache speakers with a ready means for appropriating that significance and turning it with brisk efficiency to specialized social ends. By virtue of their role as spatial anchors in traditional Apache narratives, placenames can be made to represent the narratives themselves, summarizing them, as it were, and condensing into compact form their essential moral truths. As a result, narratives and truths alike can be swiftly "activated," foregrounded, and brought into focused awareness through the use of placenames alone. And so it happens, on these occasions when Apache people see fit to speak with placenames, that a vital part of their tribal heritage seems to speak to them as well. For on such occasions, as we have seen, participants may be moved and instructed by voices other than their own. In addition, persons to whom placenames are addressed may be affected by the voice of their ancestors, a voice that communicates in compelling silence with an inherent weight described by Mikhail Bakhtin as the "authoritative word":

> The authoritative word demands that we acknowledge it, that
> we make it our own; it binds us, quite independent of any
> power it might have to persuade us internally; we encounter it
> with its authority already fused on it. The authoritative word is
> located in a distanced zone, organically connected with a past
> that is felt to be hierarchically higher. Its authority was already
> acknowledged in the past. It is a prior discourse. . . . It is given
> (it sounds) in lofty spheres, not those of familiar contact. Its
> language is a special (as it were, hieratic) language (Bakhtin
> 1981:342).

When Western Apache placenames are called upon to serve
as vehicles of ancestral authority, the wisdom thus imparted is
not so loftily given as to inhibit its utilization in the mundane
spheres of everyday life. On the contrary, as the episode at the
Machuse camp illustrates clearly, such knowledge exists to be
applied, to be thought about and acted upon, to be incorporated
(the more so the better, Lola Machuse would have us understand) into the smallest corners of personal and social experience. And insofar as this kind of incorporation occurs—insofar
as places and placenames provide Apache people with symbolic
reference points for the moral imagination and its practical
bearing on the actualities of their lives—the landscape in which
the people dwell can be said to dwell in them. For the constructions Apaches impose upon their landscape have been fashioned from the same cultural materials as constructions they
impose upon themselves as members of society. Both give expression to the same set of values, standards, and ideals; both
are manifestations of the same distinctive charter for being-in-
the-world. Inhabitants *of* their landscape, the Western Apache
are thus inhabited *by* it as well, and in the timeless depth of
that abiding reciprocity, the people and their landscape are virtually as one.

This reciprocal relationship—a relationship in which individuals invest themselves in the landscape while incorporating its meanings into their own most fundamental experience—is the ultimate source of the rich sententious potential and functional versatility of Western Apache placenames. For when placenames are used in the manner exemplified by Lola Machuse and her friends, the landscape is appropriated in pointedly social terms and the authoritative word of Apache tribal tradition is brought squarely to bear on matters of importunate social concern. Concomitantly, persons in distress are reminded of what they already know but sometimes seem to forget—that ancestral wisdom is a powerful ally in times of adversity, and that reflecting upon it, as countless generations of Apaches have learned, can produce expanded awareness, feelings of relief, and a fortified ability to cope. And because helping people to cope is regarded by Apaches as a gesture of compassion, the use of placenames for this purpose serves as well to communicate solicitude, reassurance, and personal solidarity. The primary reason that 'speaking with names' can accomplish so much—the reason its expressive force is sometimes felt to be so 'strong' (nalwod)—is that it facilitates reverberating acts of kindness and caring. And the effects of kindness and caring, especially when spirits are in need of healing, can be very strong indeed.

As must now be apparent, the ethnographic account presented in this essay has been shaped by a "pragmatic" view of spoken communication that rests on the premise that languages consist in shared economies of grammatical resources with which language users act to get things done. The resources of a language, together with the varieties of action facilitated by their use, acquire meaning and force from the sociocultural contexts in which they are embedded, and therefore, as every linguist knows, the discourse of any speech community will exhibit a fundamental character—a genius, a spirit, an underlying personality—which is very much its own. Over a period of years, I have become convinced that one of the distinctive characteristics of Western Apache discourse is a predilection for performing a maximum of socially relevant actions with a minimum of linguistic means. Accordingly, I have been drawn to investigate instances of talk, like the one involving Lola and

Robert Machuse, in which a few spoken words are made to accomplish large amounts of communicative work.[11] For it is just on such occasions, I believe, that elements of Apache culture and society fuse most completely with elements of grammar and the situated aims of individuals, such that very short utterances, like polished crystals refracting light, can be seen to contain them all. On these occasions, the Western Apache language is exploited to something near its full expressive potential, and even Apaches themselves, struck momentarily by the power of their discourse, may come away impressed.

Such powerful moments may not be commonplace in Western Apache speech communities, but they are certainly common enough—and when they occur, as on that hot and dusty day at Cibecue, robust worlds of meaning come vibrantly alive. Conveying these worlds, capturing with words both the richness of their content and the fullness of their spirit, requires an exacting effort at linguistic and cultural translation that can never be wholly successful. The problem, of course, is that verbally mediated realities are so densely textured and incorrigibly dynamic, and that one's own locutions for representing them fail to do justice to the numerous subtleties involved. Unavoidably, delicate proportions are altered and disturbed, intricate momentums halted and betrayed; and however much one explicates there is always more (or so one is tempted to suppose) that might usefully be done. Despite these persisting uncertainties, however, enough can be learned and understood so that we, like the Apache people of Cibecue, may come away from certain kinds of speech events instructed and impressed. And sometimes roundly moved. Following its more accentuated moments, moments shaped by graciousness and the resonating echoes of a fully present past, the minimalist genius of Western Apache discourse leaves us silent in its wake—traveling in our minds, listening for the ancestors, and studying the landscape with a new and different eye. On the pictorial wings of place-names imaginations soar.

Notes to Chapters

INTRODUCTION

1. A compulsive tinkerer with my own prose, I have made revisions in all of the essays included in this collection. Solely intended to enhance ease of readability and clarity of argument, the revisions do not alter in any way claims, positions, or ideas as earlier presented. Except for chapters 1 and 3, whose order has been reversed, the essays appear in the chronological sequence of their original publication.

2. Consistent with the definition proposed by the anthropologist Grenville Goodwin (1942:55), the term *Western Apache* is used to designate "Those Apachean peoples living within the present boundaries of the state of Arizona during historic times, with the exception of the Chiricahua Apache and a small band of Apaches, known as the Apache Mansos, who lived in the vicinity of Tucson." Goodwin's *The Social Organization of the Western Apache* (1942), together with his *Myths and Tales of the White Mountain Apache* (1939), provide definitive statements on these people during prereservation times. Monographs by myself—on the girls' puberty ceremonial (1966), witchcraft (1969), and a revealing form of joking (1979)—address aspects of modern Western Apache life, as does a short ethnography of the community of Cibecue (1970).

CHAPTER I
THE WESTERN APACHE CLASSIFICATORY VERB SYSTEM

Originally published in the *Southwestern Journal of Anthropology* 24(3): 252–66, 1968.

1. As in Navajo, Western Apache classificatory verb stems are distributed in neuter verbs, which denote members of the object category at rest, and active verbs, which pertain to (1) the move-

ment or handling of members of the object category, (2) the throwing or dropping of them, and (3) their free movement in space.

2. For full discussions of the procedures and steps involved in performing componential analyses, see Goodenough (1956, 1967) and Lounsbury (1956, 1964).

3. I do not claim that the analysis of Western Apache classificatory verb stem categories presented in this paper is the only one possible. Alternate "solutions" were discovered, but all of these called for the use of additional semantic dimensions and features. The solution given here is the most economical; it accounts for the data in what I believe is the simplest way possible.

4. Analysis of categories XII and XIII was strongly influenced by interpretations offered by my Apache consultants; it was they who articulated the deceptively simple dimension of ease of portability. Prior to that, I had been unable to adduce any criteria that effectively discriminated between the members of these two categories.

5. I am grateful to Brent Berlin and William Geohegan who, independently of each other, drew my attention to the fact that the semantic features employed in this analysis form an ordered sequence. An enlightening discussion of the theoretical significance of such orderings is found in Geohegan (1968).

CHAPTER 2
SEMANTIC ASPECTS OF LINGUISTIC ACCULTURATION

Originally published in *American Anthropologist* 69(5): 471–77, 1967.

1. Although it seems probable that the process of set extension has occurred in the evolution of many languages, the absence of data from nonliterate societies makes this difficult to demonstrate empirically. English scientific terminologies certainly contain extended sets (consider, for example, those found in "computerese"), and it has been suggested to me by Ward Goodenough that this is true as well of the philological languages. An interesting case of set extension, provided by an acquaintance of mine who works as an electrician, involves the extension of botanical terms to the components of complex wiring systems. According to the width of their circumference and their position relative to one another, these components are labeled "roots," "trunks," "branches," and "twigs." Appropriately enough, "roots" are "grounded." Offhand, it would appear that only a limited amount of set extension occurs in modern colloquial American English, in part because of the ease with which old words are dismantled and recombined to provide

fresh labels for new ideas and inventions. More important, perhaps, is that owing to the unceasing efforts of advertising agencies, new items come with names already attached. This, of course, would discourage set extensions.

CHAPTER 3
A WESTERN APACHE WRITING SYSTEM

Originally published in *Science* 180(4090): 1013–22, 1973.

1. I have adopted I. J. Gelb's (1963:12) broad definition of writing as "a system of human intercommunication by means of conventional visible marks." The Silas John system is a script because it consists of phonetic signs.

2. References to the impact of the Silas John movement upon Western Apache and Mescalero Apache religions are not infrequent, but a systematic appraisal of the cultural and historical factors that precipitated its appearance and acceptance has yet to be made. The earliest example of the Silas John script consists of two prayer texts recorded by Harry Hoijer on the Mescalero reservation in New Mexico during the summer of 1931. A number of symbols that occur in Hoijer's Mescalero texts are absent from those we collected at San Carlos (and vice versa), and at present we do not know whether these symbols represent innovations by the Mescalero or whether they originally appeared in Western Apache texts not included in our sample.

3. The terms *etic* and *emic* are used in this paper to refer to contrasting types of anthropological description. A description of a linguistic or cultural system is emic to the extent that it is based on distinctions that are demonstrably meaningful and functionally significant for competent users of the system. A description is etic to the extent that it rests upon distinctions (typically drawn from cross-cultural typologies) whose meaningfulness for a particular system's users has not been demonstrated and whose functional significance within the system is therefore open to question. For an extended discussion of the etic/emic distinction and its implications, see Goodenough (1970).

4. For example, we were unable to record the full inventory of symbols used by Silas John to write his sixty-two original prayers.

5. "Power" is the power God confers upon those who truly believe in him.

6. "Harmful knowledge" refers to the body of techniques employed by 'witches' (*'iłgashń*) to cause sickness and misfortune. For a description of some of these techniques, see Basso (1969).

7. This is the ritual name of Silas John. It is spoken only during the performance of ceremonials.

8. In all rituals associated with the Silas John religion, the phrase *hádndín 'ishkiin* ('pollen boy') refers metaphorically to male ceremonial patients. If the patient is female, the phrase is modified accordingly to *hádndín na'ilihn* ('pollen girl').

9. In all the prayers we collected, the term *ndee* ('man', 'men') is used in the general sense of "all men" or "mankind."

10. Cattail pollen is the foremost symbol in the Silas John religion of God and Jesus and their spiritual presence on this earth.

11. Like God and Jesus, pollen is construed as having life.

12. Pollen, a symbol of God, has life. To live is to breathe, hence the equation of pollen with the breath of God.

CHAPTER 4
'WISE WORDS' OF THE WESTERN APACHE

Originally published in *Meaning in Anthropology*, Keith Basso and Harry Selby, eds., pp. 98–123. University of New Mexico Press, Albuquerque, 1976.

1. Since the appearance of this essay in 1976, linguists and philosophers have become increasingly interested in the topic of metaphor, and Chomsky's conception of semantic theory has been challenged on several fronts. Most notably, Lakoff and Johnson (1980) have presented convincing evidence that metaphor plays a fundamental role in organizing patterns of thought, and Lakoff (1988) has developed a theory of linguistic meaning, different from Chomsky's in essential repects, which purports to explain how this is so. Although the efforts of these and other writers are to be applauded, their inclination to work only with metaphors drawn from English—and also to avoid any serious consideration of the situated uses to which metaphors may actually be put—seems to me to be unfortunate. I continue to believe that an adequate understanding of the meaning of figurative speech must openly embrace its complex cultural underpinnings, its rich expressive potential, and its widely acknowledged value as an unrivaled resource for accomplishing particular forms of social interaction.

CHAPTER 5
'TO GIVE UP ON WORDS'

Originally published in *Southwestern Journal of Anthropology* 26(3): 213–30, 1970.

1. The social situations described in this paper are not the only ones in which Western Apaches regularly refrain from speech.

There is a second set of situations in which silence appears to occur solely as a gesture of respect, usually to persons in a position of authority. A third set involves ritual specialists who claim they must keep silent at certain points during the preparation of ceremonial paraphernalia.

2. I would like to stress that the emphasis placed here on social relations is fully in keeping with the Western Apache interpretation of their own behavior. When my consultants were asked to explain why they or someone else was silent on a particular occasion, they invariably did so in terms of *who* was present at the time.

CHAPTER 6
'STALKING WITH STORIES'

Originally published in *Text, Play, and Story: The Reconstruction of Self and Society*, Eduard Bruner, ed., pp. 19–55. American Anthropological Association, Washington, D.C., 1984.

1. A prominent figure in Western Apache oral literature, Slim Coyote is appreciated by Apache people for his keen and crafty intelligence, his complex and unpredictable personality, and his penchant for getting himself into difficult situations from which he always manages to extract himself, usually with humorous and embarrassing results. Short collections of Western Apache Coyote tales may be found in Goddard (1919) and Goodwin (1939).

2. One consequence of this neglect is that few North American Indian groups today possess maps representing the lands that formerly belonged to them. This has become a source of major concern to Indian people, especially in their dealings with state and federal governments. As Vine Deloria, Jr. (personal communication, 1981), has observed, "To name the land was for many Indians a way of claiming it, a way that proved more than adequate until Europeans arrived and started to claim the land for themselves with considerably harsher methods. Now, in litigation over the land, Indian claims can be disputed (and sometimes rejected) because many of the old names that marked tribal boundaries have been forgotten and lost."

3. Other aspects of the Western Apache placename system are treated in Basso (1983).

4. Jokes of this type are intended to poke fun at the butt of the joke and, at the same time, to comment negatively on the interactional practices of Anglo-Americans. An extended discussion of this form of Western Apache humor is presented in Basso (1979).

CHAPTER 7
'SPEAKING WITH NAMES'

Originally published in *Cultural Anthropology* 3(2): 99–130, 1988.

1. Compatible views on environmental appropriation are expressed in Deloria (1975) and Silko (1986).

2. Silverstein (1976, 1979) argues that a preoccupation with the "semantico-referential" function of language has provided the basis for a uniquely biased Western linguistic ideology in which other functions, especially indexical ones, are accorded secondary importance. In this regard, the views expressed in Tyler (1978, 1984) are also highly instructive.

3. Emily and Louise are pseudonyms; Lola Machuse, Robert Machuse, and Clifford are not.

4. This verbal exchange was not recorded on tape. I am satisfied, however, as are the Apache persons who participated in the exchange, that the text given here is essentially accurate. What is missing, of course, is information pertaining to prosodic phenomena, but none of the participants could recall anything in this regard that they considered out of the ordinary. Lola Machuse offered the following generalization: "When we talk like that [i.e., 'speaking with names'] we just talk soft and slow, so that people know to listen real good."

5. I follow here Silverstein's (1979:195) definition of linguistic ideologies as "any sets of beliefs about language as a rationalization or justification of perceived language structure and use." For an informative discussion of some of the perceptual and cognitive limits that may be inherent in linguistic ideologies, see Silverstein (1981).

6. Refraining from speaking too much has pleasing aesthetic consequences that Apache people from Cibecue value and appreciate. It produces a lean narrative style, concise and somewhat stark, which is notably free of cursory embellishments—a kind of narrative minimalism in which less is held to be more. But it is a narrative style with definite moral underpinnings. Refraining from speaking too much results in effective depictions, and this, Apaches say, is all to the good. But economical speech also shows respect for the ample picturing abilities of other people, and this is better still.

7. The pictorial character of Western Apache placenames is frequently remarked upon when Apache people are asked to compare their own placenames with familiar placenames in English. On

such occasions, English names—such as Globe, Show Low, Mc-
Nary, Phoenix, and others—are regularly found deficient for "not
showing what those places look like" or for "not letting you see
those places in your mind." Alternatively, Western Apache placenames—such as *gizh yaa'itin* ('trail leads down through a gap between two hills'), *ch'iłdiiyé cho sikaad* ('cluster of big walnut trees
stands bushing out'), and *túzhį' yaahichii* ('redness spreads out extending down to water')—are consistently praised for "making you
see those places like they really are" or for "putting those places in
your mind so you can see them after you go away." One Apache
from Cibecue put the difference succinctly: "The Whiteman's
names [are] no good. They don't give pictures to your mind." And a
local wit said this: "Apaches don't need Polaroids. We've got good
names!"

8. The distinguishing features of these three traditional narrative genres as articulated by Western Apache people themselves are
discussed in chapter 6.

9. Western Apaches readily acknowledge that 'speaking with
names' is possible only among persons who share knowledge of the
same traditional narratives; otherwise, placenames would evoke
stories for hearers that are different from those intended by speakers. But this, it seems, is rarely a problem among older people. Most
adults living in Cibecue maintain that they are familiar with the
same corpus of narratives, and while any narrative is understood to
have several versions (and different storytellers different ways of
performing them), there is little confusion as to where events in
the narrative are believed to have taken place. Consequently, the
placename (or placenames) that anchor a narrative can function re-
liably to evoke comparable images of ancestral events and corre-
sponding appreciations of ancestral wisdom. Younger Apache people, I was told, are ignorant of both placenames and traditional
narratives in increasing numbers, so that for some of them 'speaking with names' has become difficult or impossible. Although the
instance of 'speaking with names' discussed in the present essay
features women conversing with women, I have been assured by
consultants from Cibecue that the use of this verbal practice has
never been, and is not today, restricted to female interlocutors.
Apache men, I was informed, employ the practice when speaking
to men, and persons of opposite sex may employ it when speaking
to each other.

10. Louise, who is distantly related to Emily, is not related to
Lola Machuse or Robert Machuse.

11. This view of language and its suitability for an ethnographic

approach to the study of discourse has been most fully articulated by Hymes (1974). For extended applications of this approach, together with useful theoretical discussion, see Sherzer (1983) and Bauman (1984). Hymes's more recent work (1981) is also illustrative in this regard, as are treatments by Bauman (1986), Feld (1982), and Friedrich (1986). Tyler (1978) presents a sweeping philosophical critique of formalism in modern linguistic theory and, on grounds somewhat different than Hymes, argues persuasively for a more sensitive and sensible approach to the study of language use in its cultural and social contexts.

References Cited

ALSTON, W.
1964 *Philosophy of Language*. Englewood Cliffs: Prentice-Hall.

BAKHTIN, M.
1981 *The Dialogic Imagination: Four Essays by M. M. Bakhtin*. M. Holquist, ed. Austin: University of Texas Press.

BASSO, K.
1966 *The Gift of Changing Woman*. Bureau of American Ethnology Bulletin 196. Washington, D.C.: Smithsonian Institution.

1969 *Western Apache Witchcraft*. Anthropological Papers of the University of Arizona 15. Tucson: University of Arizona Press.

1970 *The Cibecue Apache*. New York: Holt, Rinehart and Winston.

1979 *Portraits of the "Whiteman": Linguistic Play and Cultural Symbols among the Western Apache*. Cambridge: Cambridge University Press.

1983 Western Apache Placename Hierarchies. In *Naming Systems. 1981 Proceedings of the American Ethnological Society*. E. Tooker, ed., pp. 37–46. Washington, D.C.: American Ethnological Society.

BAUMAN, R.
1984 *Verbal Art as Performance*. Chicago: Waveland Press.

1986 *Story, Performance, and Event: Contextual Studies of Oral Narrative*. Cambridge: Cambridge University Press.

BECKER, A.
1982 Beyond Translation: Esthetics and Language Description. In *Contemporary Perceptions of Language: Interdisciplinary Dimensions*. H. Byrnes, ed., pp. 124–37. Washington, D.C.: Georgetown University Press.

184 /   *References Cited*

BEVER, T., AND P. ROSENBAUM
  1971 Some Lexical Structures and Their Empirical Validity. In *Semantics*. D. Steinberg and L. Jakobovits, eds., pp. 586–89. Cambridge: Cambridge University Press.
BLACK, M.
  1962 *Models and Metaphors.* Ithaca: Cornell University Press.
BOAS, F.
  1901–07 *The Eskimo of Baffin Land and Hudson Bay.* Bulletin of the American Museum of Natural History 15. New York.
  1934 *Geographical Names of the Kwakiutl Indians.* Columbia University Contributions in Anthropology No. 20. New York.
BRÉAL, M.
  1964 *Semantics: Studies in the Science of Meaning.* New York: Dover.
BROWN, R., AND A. GILMAN
  1960 The Pronouns of Power and Solidarity. In *Style in Language*. T. Sebeok, ed., pp. 253–76. Cambridge, Mass.: MIT Press.
CARNAP, R.
  1955 *Philosophy and Logical Syntax.* London: Routledge and Kegan Paul.
CHOMSKY, N.
  1965 *Aspects of the Theory of Syntax.* Cambridge, Mass.: MIT Press.
CSIKSZENTMIHALYI, M., AND E. ROCHBERG-HALTON
  1981 *The Meaning of Things: Domestic Symbols and the Self.* Cambridge: Cambridge University Press.
DAVIDSON, W., L. ELFORT, AND H. HOIJER
  1963 Athapaskan Classificatory Verbs. In *Studies in the Athapaskan Languages*. H. Hoijer, ed., pp. 30–41. University of California Publications in Linguistics 29. Berkeley.
DE LAGUNA, F.
  1972 *Under Mount St. Elias: The History and Culture of the Yakotat Tlingit.* Smithsonian Contributions to Anthropology 7. Washington, D.C.: Smithsonian Institution.
DELORIA, V., JR.
  1975 *God is Red.* New York: Dell.
ELIOT, T.
  1932 *The Sacred Wood.* London: Methuen.
ERVIN-TRIPP, S.
  1967 *Sociolinguistics.* Language-Behavior Research Laboratory

Working Paper 3. Berkeley: University of California.

FELD, S.
1982 *Sound and Sentiment: Birds, Weeping, Poetics, and Song in Kaluli Expression.* Philadelphia: University of Pennsylvania Press.

FRAKE, C.
1962 The Ethnographic Study of Cognitive Systems. In *Anthropology and Human Behavior.* T. Gladwin and W. Sturtevant, eds., pp. 72–85. Washington, D.C.: Washington Anthropological Society.
1964 How to Ask for a Drink in Subanun. In *The Ethnography of Communication.* J. Gumperz and D. Hymes, eds., pp. 86–102. *American Anthropologist* 66(6, part 2).

FRIEDRICH, P.
1966 Structural Implications of Russian Pronomial Usage. In *Sociolinguistics.* W. Bright, ed., pp. 214–53. The Hague: Mouton.
1986 *The Language Parallax: Linguistic Relativism and Poetic Indeterminacy.* Austin: University of Texas Press.

GALLICO, P.
1954 *Love of Seven Dolls and Other Stories.* New York: Doubleday.

GEERTZ, C.
1964 Ideology as a Cultural System. In *Ideology and Discontent.* D. Apter, ed., pp. 47–76. Glencoe, Ill.: Free Press.
1973 Thick Description: Toward an Interpretive Theory of Culture. In *The Interpretation of Cultures: Selected Essays by Clifford Geertz,* pp. 3–30. New York: Basic Books.

GELB, I.
1963 *A Study of Writing.* Chicago: University of Chicago Press.

GEOHEGAN, W.
1968 *Information Processing Systems in Culture.* Language-Behavior Research Laboratory Working Paper 6. Berkeley: University of California.

GODDARD, P.
1919 *Myths and Tales from the White Mountain Apache.* Anthropological Publications of the American Museum of Natural History 24. New York.

GOFFMAN, E.
1961 *Encounters: Two Studies in the Sociology of Interaction.* Indianapolis: Bobbs-Merrill.
1963 *Behavior in Public Places.* Glencoe, Ill.: Free Press.

1974   *Frame Analysis: An Essay in the Organization of Experience.* New York: Harper and Row.

GOODENOUGH, W.

1956   Componential Analysis and the Study of Meaning. *Language* 32:195–216.

1967   Componential Analysis. *Science* 156:1203–9.

1970   *Description and Comparison in Cultural Anthropology.* Chicago: Aldine.

GOODWIN, G.

1939   *Myths and Tales of the White Mountain Apache.* Memoirs of the American Folklore Society 33.

1942   *The Social Organization of the Western Apache.* Chicago: University of Chicago Press.

GREENBIE, B.

1981   *Spaces: Dimensions of the Human Landscape.* New Haven: Yale University Press.

GUMPERZ, J.

1961   Speech Variation and the Study of Indian Civilization. *American Anthropologist* 63:976–88.

HAAS, M.

1967   Language and Taxonomy in Northern California. *American Anthropologist* 69:358–62.

HAMMEL, E.

1964   Introduction. In *Formal Semantic Analysis.* E. A. Hammel, ed., pp. 1–8. *American Anthropologist* 67(5, part 2).

HARRINGTON, J.

1916   *The Ethnogeography of the Tewa Indians.* Annual Report of the Bureau of American Ethnology 29. Washington, D.C.

HAUGEN, E.

1956   *The Norwegian Language in America: A Study of Bilingual Behavior.* Philadelphia: University of Pennsylvania Press.

HEANY, S.

1980   *Preoccupations: Selected Prose 1968–1978.* London: Faber and Faber.

HEIDEGGER, M.

1977   Building Dwelling Thinking. In *Martin Heidegger: Basic Writings.* D. Krell, ed., pp. 319–39. New York: Harper and Row.

HENLE, P.

1962   *Language, Thought, and Culture.* Ann Arbor: University of Michigan Press.

HERZOG, G.

1941 Culture Change and Language: Shifts in Pima Vocabulary. In *Language, Culture, and Personality*. L. Spier, A. I. Hallowell, and S. Newman, eds., pp. 51–65. Menasha, Wisconsin.

HILL, F.

1963 Some Comparisons between San Carlos and White Mountain Dialects of Western Apache. In *Studies of the Athapaskan Languages*. H. Hoijer, ed., pp. 87–97. University of California Publications in Linguistics 29. Berkeley.

HOIJER, H.

1945 Classificatory Verb Stems in the Apachean Languages. *International Journal of Linguistics* 11:13–23.

HYMES, D.

1962 The Ethnography of Speaking. In *Anthropology and Human Behavior*. T. Gladwin and W. Sturtevant, eds., pp. 13–53. Washington, D.C.: Washington Anthropological Society.

1964 Introduction: Toward Ethnographies of Communication. In *The Ethnography of Communication*. J. Gumperz and D. Hymes, eds., pp. 1–34. *American Anthropologist* 66(6, part 2).

1967 Models of the Interaction of Language and Social Setting. *Social Forces* 23:8–28.

1971 Sociolinguistics and the Ethnography of Speaking. In *Social Anthropology and Language*. E. Ardener, ed., pp. 47–93. London: Tavistock.

1972 Models of the Interaction of Language and Social Life. In *Directions in Sociolinguistics*. J. Gumperz and D. Hymes, eds., pp. 35–71. New York: Holt, Rinehart and Winston.

1973 *Toward Linguistic Competence*. Texas Working Papers in Sociolinguistics 16. Austin: Southwest Educational Development Laboratory.

1974 *Foundations in Sociolinguistics: An Ethnographic Approach*. Philadelphia: University of Pennsylvania Press.

1981 *In Vain I Tried to Tell You: Essays in Native American Ethnopoetics*. Philadelphia: University of Pennsylvania Press.

KATZ, J.

1972 *Semantic Theory*. New York: Harper and Row.

KATZ, J., AND J. FODOR

1963 The Structure of a Semantic Theory. *Language* 39:170–210.

KLUCKHOHN, C.

1949   *Mirror for Man.* New York: McGraw-Hill.

LABOV, W., AND D. FANSHEL

1977   *Therapeutic Discourse: Psychotherapy as Conversation.* New York: Academic Press.

LAKOFF, G.

1988   *Women, Fire, and Dangerous Things: What Categories Reveal about the Mind.* Chicago: University of Chicago Press.

LAKOFF, G., AND M. JOHNSON

1980   *Metaphors We Live By.* Chicago: University of Chicago Press.

LOUNSBURY, F.

1956   A Semantic Analysis of the Pawnee Kinship Usage. *Language* 32:158–94.

1960   Iroquois Place-names in the Champlain Valley. In *Report of the New York-Vermont Interstate Commission on Lake Champlain Basin.* New York Legislative Document 9, pp. 21–66. Albany.

1964   The Structural Analysis of Kinship Semantics. In *Proceedings of the Ninth International Congress of Linguists.* H. G. Lunt, ed., pp. 1073–93. The Hague: Mouton.

MALLERY, G.

1888–89   Picture-Writing of the American Indians. In *Tenth Annual Report of the Bureau of American Ethnology,* pp. 3–822. Washington, D.C.: U.S. Government Printing Office.

MERLEAU-PONTY, M.

1969   On the Phenomenology of Language. In *Problems in the Philosophy of Language.* T. Dishewsky, ed., pp. 89–101. New York: Holt, Rinehart and Winston.

MOMADAY, N. SCOTT

1974   Native American Attitudes to the Environment. In *Seeing with a Native Eye: Essays on Native American Religion.* W. Capps, ed., pp. 79–85. New York: Harper and Row.

MOWRER, P.

1970   Notes on Navajo Silence Behavior. Unpublished manuscript. University of Arizona, Tucson.

PERCY, W.

1958   Metaphor as Mistake. *Sewanee Review* 66:79–99.

RADIN, P.

1916   *The Winnebago Tribe.* Annual Report of the Bureau of American Ethnology 37. Washington, D.C.

READ, H.
1952 *English Prose Style.* London: G. Bell and Sons.

RICOEUR, P.
1979 The Model of the Text: Meaningful Action Considered as a Text. In *Interpretive Social Science: A Reader.* P. Rabinow and W. Sullivan, eds., pp. 92–123. Berkeley: University of California Press.

SAPIR, E.
1912 Language and Environment. *American Anthropologist* 14:226–42.

SHERZER, J.
1983 *Kuna Ways of Speaking: An Ethnographic Perspective.* Austin: University of Texas Press.

SHIBLES, W.
1971 *An Analysis of Metaphor in Light of W. A. Urban's Theories.* The Hague: Mouton and Co.

SILKO, L.
1981 Language and Literature from a Pueblo Indian Perspective. In *Opening up the Cañon.* L. Fiedler and H. Baker, trans. and eds., pp. 54–72. Baltimore: Johns Hopkins University Press.
1986 Landscape, History, and the Pueblo Imagination. In *Antaeus, Special Issue: On Nature.* D. Halpern, ed., pp. 85–94. New York: Ecco Press.

SILVERSTEIN, M.
1976 Shifters, Linguistic Categories, and Cultural Description. In *Meaning in Anthropology.* K. Basso and H. Selby, eds., pp. 11–53. Albuquerque: University of New Mexico Press.
1979 Language Structure and Linguistic Ideology. In *The Elements: A Parasession on Linguistic Units and Levels.* P. Clyne, W. Hanks, and C. Hofbauer, eds., pp. 193–247. Chicago: University of Chicago Press.
1981 *The Limits of Awareness.* Texas Working Papers in Sociolinguistics 84. Austin: Southwest Educational Development Laboratory.

TEETER, K.
1970 Review of Leonard Bloomfield's *The Menominee Language. Language* 46:524–33.

TRAGER, G.
1968 Whorf, Benjamin L. In *International Encyclopedia of the Social Sciences,* Vol. 16. D. Sills, ed., pp. 536–37. New York: Cromwell Collier and MacMillan.

TYLER, S.

1978 *The Said and the Unsaid: Mind, Meaning, and Culture.* New York: Academic Press.

1984 The Vision in the Quest, or What the Mind's Eye Sees. *Journal of Anthropological Research* 40:23–40.

ULLMAN, S.

1962 *Semantics: An Introduction to the Science of Meaning.* New York: Barnes and Noble.

1963 *The Principles of Semantics.* New York: Barnes and Noble.

URBAN, W.

1939 *Language and Reality.* London: George Allen and Unwin.

WALDRON, R.

1967 *Sense and Sense Development.* London: Andre Deutsch, The Language Library.

WEINREICH, U.

1953 *Languages in Contact.* New York: Linguistic Circle of New York.

1966 Explorations in Semantic Theory. In *Current Trends in Linguistics,* T. Sebeok, ed., vol. 3, pp. 395–477. The Hague: Mouton and Co.

Index

Acculturation: linguistic, 22, 23–24
Actions: metaphor in, 65–67; writing symbols for, 46–47, 49–50, 51
Allographs, 47–58
Anatomical terms: for automobiles, 18–21, 22; extension of, 17–18, 23–24
Ancestors: authority of, 170–71; placenames and, 156, 157–58
Anger: and silence, 88–90
Athabaskan languages: verb system of, 1, 2
Attributes: of metaphor construction, 64–65
Automobiles: anatomical terms for, 18–21, 22, 23

Bakhtin, Mikhail, 128, 171
Becker, Alton, 169
Behavior: in anger, 88–90; in grief, 90–92; nonverbal, 39, 45–49; silence as, 82, 94–95
Boarding schools, 87–88
Boas, Franz, 105, 106

Camps, 83
Carnap, Rudolph, 55
Categories, 32, 63, 114 (fig.), 115 (fig.); definition of, 2–4, 8–11;
of foreign terms, 23–24; of placenames, 106, 110–12; semantic, 7–9, 55, 71; verb stem, 4–7
Ceremony, 83; instructions in, 49–50; material culture in, 45–47; silence during, 92–94, 97
Children: communication with parents by, 87–88, 95
Chomsky, Noam, 73, 76–77, 78–79, 178n.1
Cibecue: placenames around, 106–8; social groups in, 82–83
Clans, 83. See also Kinship; Relationships
Classification, 114; of foreign terms, 23–24; linguistic, 1–2; of symbols, 50–51; system extension, 18, 22; verb stem, 4–7
Codes, 81; for nonverbal behavior, 45–49
Communication, 81, 96; conservation in, 172–73; in curing ceremonies, 93–94; about land, 141–42; with placenames, 170–71
Competence: linguistic, 76–78
Connotative features: of grammar, 75–76; of metaphors, 63–68, 74–75
Constituents: of metaphors, 62, 64

Contact: intercultural, 15, 16
Conversation, 153; communica-
    tion in, 172–73; purpose of,
    150–51; social functions of,
    169–70; understanding, 146–
    48, 170, 180n.4; unspoken
    meaning in, 167–68
Courtesy: in speech, 153–54
Courtship: silence during, 85–
    86, 97
Coyote stories, 114, 179n.1
Craziness: in anger, 89–90; in
    grief, 91–92
Creativity: and metaphor, 55, 71,
    78
Curing ceremony: power in,
    92–94

Definition by signification, 3
Definition by typification, 2
Deloria, Vine, Jr., 130
Denotata, 3; of verb stems, 4–7
Depiction, 173; of placenames,
    155–58; in speech, 152–54,
    180–81nn.6, 7

East Fork, 29
Edwards, Silas John, 178n.7; writ-
    ing system of, 26, 29–31. *See
    also* Silas John movement;
    Silas John prayer texts
Elements: of symbols, 35, 37–38
Emic typology, 177n.3; of writing
    system, 27–28, 50
Environment, 103, 106; Ameri-
    can Indians and, 130–31, 132–
    33, 136–37
Errors, 77
Ethnography, 55, 81, 99–100, 136
Etic typology, 177n.3; of writing
    systems, 27, 28–29, 50

Families, 83. *See also* Kinship;
    Relationships

Geertz, Clifford, 53, 62, 72
Geography. *See* Land; Placenames
Goodenough, Ward, 28
Gossip, 144–45; stories related
    to, 114, 116
Grammar, 73, 74; connotative
    meanings of, 75–76; of place-
    names, 108–10; rules and in-
    formation in, 76–77. *See also*
    Transformational grammar
Graphs: in writing systems,
    26–27
Grief: and silence, 90–92, 97

Harjo, Joy, 130
Harrington, J. P., 106
Healing: in historical stories,
    125–26; speaking with names
    in, 160–61
Heidegger, Martin, 141
Herzog, George, 22
Historical tales, 114, 115; im-
    pacts of, 124–31; individual fo-
    cus of, 121–23; placenames in,
    116–17; social behavior in,
    117–20; social functions of,
    163–67
Hoijer, Harry, 107–8, 154
Hunting: as metaphor, 123, 124–
    25, 126–27, 135
Hymes, Dell, 53, 77–78, 81

Ideographs, 27
Imagination, 171; in conversa-
    tion, 153–54, 173; and place-
    names, 142, 155–56, 160, 180–
    81n.7
Information: figurative, 75–76;
    nonsemantic, 74–75; seman-
    tic, 73–74
Invention, 77

Katz, Jerrold, 73–74
Kinetic signs, 52

Kinship, 97; consanguineal, 82–83
Kluckhohn, Clyde, 99

Laguna, 130
Laguna, Frederica de, 106
Land, 149, 179n.2; concepts about, 100–1, 102, 133–34; moral symbolism of, 126–31; relationship to, 171–72; significance of, 138–40; and social behavior, 142–43; social construct of, 140–41; and social relationships, 141–42. *See also* Placenames
Language, 76, 152
Lewis, Benson, 119
Lexemes, 16, 51, 70; extension of, 17–19, 21–24
Lexical gaps, 69, 71
Loanwords, 16
Logographs, 50
Lounsbury, Floyd, 106

Machuse, Lola: on conversation, 146, 147, 148, 149, 150–51, 161, 164, 165–68
Mallery, Garrick, 25
Material culture: used in ritual, 45–47
Meanings: connotative, 56, 61, 68; designative, 56, 61–62; discovering, 57–58
Medicine men, 115; power of, 92–93
Medicine women, 115
Memory, 160. *See also* Imagination
Metalanguage, 13
Metaphor(s), 53, 69, 75, 134; connotative features of, 63–68; as creative activity, 71–72; cultural interpretation of, 55–58; explanatory, 59–61; functions

of, 68, 135; of hunting, 123, 124–25, 126–27, 135; interpretation of, 65, 71, 136; linguistic competence and, 77–78; principles of, 63–64; theoretical models of, 53, 178n.1; transformational grammar and, 78–79; Western Apache, 58–59. *See also* Wise words
Momaday, N. Scott, 130, 142
Morality, 134, 148, 170; teaching, 127, 128
Morphology: of placenames, 108–10
Mourning. *See* Grief
Mowrer, Priscilla, 96–97
Myths, 114, 115, 116

Names: linguistic function of, 70, 143–44; speaking with, 151, 158–60, 169–70, 172, 181n.9. *See also* Placenames
Narratives: classification of, 114–15. *See also* Gossip; Historical tales; Myths; Sagas; Storytelling
Navajo culture: placenames in, 107—8; silence in, 96–97
Navajo language, 2

Objects: classification of, 1–2, 23–24; relationships of, 11, 12
Ortiz, Alfonso, 130
Ortiz, Simon, 130

Paraphrases: explanatory, 59–61
Parents: communication with children by, 87–88, 95
Participants: in social situations, 95–96
Patients: in curing ceremonies, 92, 93, 94, 97
Peaches, Annie, 118, 127
Percy, Walker, 55

Performance. *See* Ceremony
Phraseographs, 50–51
Pictographs, 27
Piman language, 22
Placenames, 104; American Indian, 105–6; categories of, 110–12; around Cibecue, 106—8; in communication, 146, 147, 148; depiction of, 170, 180–81n.7; functions of, 144, 154–59, 160–61; in historical tales, 116–17, 118, 119, 120, 126; importance of, 172, 179n.2; morphology of, 108–10; social contexts of, 143, 181n.9; speaking with, 151, 158–60, 162–63, 169–71, 173; in storytelling, 112–13, 154
Places, 141, 142; human interaction with, 139–40
Power: in curing ceremonies, 92–94; of places, 100, 101, 148
Prayers: writing system for, 26, 29–30. *See also* Prayer texts
Prayer texts, 32–34 (figs.), 178n.9; instructions in, 39–40, 49–50; nonverbal behavior, 45–47; symbols in, 40, 48–49

Read, Herbert, 58
Relationships: establishing, 94–95; with land, 132–33, 134, 141–42, 171–72; and silence, 83–84, 94; social identities and, 95–96
Relatives. *See* Kinship; Relationships
Residences, 83
Rituals. *See* Ceremony
Rules: linguistic, 63, 76

Sadness. *See* Grief
Sagas, 114, 115–16
Sapir, Edward, 105–6
Seduction tales, 114

Self: claims about, 99–100; historical tales and, 121–23, 124–31; and land, 100–2
Semantic change: documenting, 15–16
Semantic dimensions, 12 (fig.); sets of, 13–14; of verb stems, 7–11
Semantics, 62, 180n.2; goals of, 53–54; in transformational grammar, 73–74. *See also* Semantic change; Semantic dimensions; Semantic theory
Semantic theory, 178n.1; goals of, 73–74
Set extension, 22–23, 176–77n.1
Significata, 3
Signs: kinetic, 52; phonetic, 50, 51–52; phonetic-kinetic, 52; phonetic nonsemantic, 50; phonetic semantic, 50–51
Silas John. *See* Edwards, Silas John; Silas John movement; Silas John prayer texts
Silas John movement: 177n.2, 178nn.7, 8, 10
Silas John prayer texts, 177n.2; analysis of, 31–40; compound symbols in, 42–45; noncompound symbols in, 41–42; nonverbal behavior in, 45–49
Silence, 80, 98, 178–79nn.1, 2; and anger, 88–90; as appropriate behavior, 94–95, 96; during courtship, 85–86; functions of, 81–82; and grief, 90–92; and interpersonal relationships, 83–94; in Navajo culture, 96–97; among parents and children, 87–88
Silko, Leslie, M., 130
Simile, 56
Sings, 97; power in, 92–94
Social behavior, 148, 179n.21; acceptable, 103, 126; comment-

ing on, 167–68; controlling, 124–25, 126–27, 129, 163; historical tales and, 117–23, 163–67; and land, 142–43; speaking with names and, 161–62, 163–66
Social groups: and interpersonal relationships, 82–83
Social identities: and relationships, 95–96
Social structure: and environment, 133, 141–42
Speech, 77, 85, 114, 135; among children and parents, 87–88; as cooperative activity, 148–49; courtesy in, 153–54, 180n.6; depiction in, 152–53; with placenames, 151, 158–60; significance of, 139–40; and silence, 81–82
Stimulus diffusion, 26
Storytelling, 180n.6; function of, 162–63; as hunting, 123, 124–25, 135; of land and individuals, 102–3, 130; placenames in, 112–13, 154–55, 157, 158, 170–71. *See also* Historical tales; Myths; Sagas
Strangers: speaking with, 84–85, 95
Symbolism: of land, 100–2, 114, 132
Symbols, 40; classification of, 27–28, 50–51; compound, 37–39, 42–45, 48–49, 51; discrimination among, 35, 37; elements of, 35, 37; graphic, 26–27; noncompound, 41–42, 46–47, 48–49, 51; in Silas John texts, 29–30, 31–40; in writing systems, 26–27, 50–52

Taxonomies: cultural, 1, 2; extended, 19, 20–21 (figs.), 22
Terminology: extended meanings of, 17–18

Thompson, Nick, 103, 132, 137; on placenames, 104–5; on storytelling, 113–14, 120, 124–25, 126
Thought: and conversation, 153–54
Time: in narrative genres, 114–15
Topography. *See* Land; Placenames
Toponyms. *See* Placenames
Trager, George, 141
Transformational grammar, 53–54, 76; components of, 72–73; metaphor in, 78–79; nonsemantic information in, 74–75; semantic information in, 73–74

Vehicles: classification of, 23–24
Verbs: classification of, 3–4. *See also* Verb stems
Verb stems: category definition of, 2–4, 13; classificatory, 1–2, 175–76nn.1, 3; definitions of, 8–11; denotata of, 4–7; relationships of, 11, 13; semantic dimensions of, 7–8
Vision: and language, 152–53
Vocabulary, 68; and intercultural contact, 15, 16
Vocalization, 39

Waldron, R. A., 62–63
Weinreich, Uriel, 74–75
Wise words, 59, 65, 68, 77. *See also* Metaphor(s)
Writing systems, 40, 177n.1; access to, 30–31; American Indian, 25–26, 52; compound symbols in, 42–45; descriptions of, 26–27; development of, 29–31; emic analysis of, 28–29; noncompound symbols in, 41–42; symbols in, 27–28, 39, 50–52

ABOUT THE AUTHOR

Keith H. Basso began linguistic and ethnographic fieldwork among the Western Apache as a sophomore in college in 1959. He has continued this research ever since, mainly in the community of Cibecue on the Fort Apache Indian reservation in east-central Arizona. Formerly professor of anthropology at Yale University and the University of Arizona, he now teaches alternate semesters at the University of New Mexico. Mr. Basso has served as president of the American Ethnological Society, Editor for Linguistics of *American Anthropologist,* and as a member of the board of directors of the Association on American Indian Affairs. At the request of the White Mountain and San Carlos Apache tribes, he has also given expert testimony in a number of state and federal legal proceedings involving tribal members. When not engaged in teaching, Mr. Basso lives with his wife, Gayle Potter-Basso, on a ranch in northern Arizona. There he writes, marvels at the doings of coyotes and hawks, and does what he can to improve the reputation of mules.